# Executricks

ALSO BY STANLEY BING

NONFICTION

*Biz Words*

*What Would Machiavelli Do?*

*Throwing the Elephant*

*Sun Tzu Was a Sissy*

*The Big Bing*

*Rome, Inc.*

*100 Bullshit Jobs . . . And How to Get Them*

*Crazy Bosses*

FICTION

*Lloyd: What Happened*

*You Look Nice Today*

**Collins**

*An Imprint of* HarperCollins*Publishers*

# Executricks

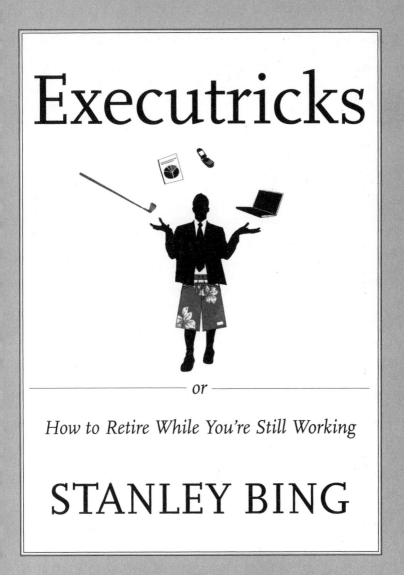

*or*

*How to Retire While You're Still Working*

# STANLEY BING

HarperCollins books may be purchased for educational, business, or sales promotional use. For information, please write: Special Markets Department, HarperCollins Publishers, 10 East 53rd Street, New York, NY 10022.

FIRST EDITION

Designed by Jaime Putorti

Library of Congress Cataloging-in-Publication Data is available upon request.

ISBN-13: 978-0-06-134035-2

08   09   10   11   12   WBC/RRD   10   9   8   7   6   5   4   3   2   1

*To Laura*

# Contents

# Executricks

# Enter the Executrick

Ah me, we think. What to do? On the one hand, I'm getting too old for this stuff. And I felt this way about six minutes after I got my first business card. I didn't go into business to work hard. I did this to make money. Then somewhere along the line I got to be the guy who has to do everything. It's like in a bank. You look at the tellers and they're busting their humps. Somewhere behind them there's a guy in an inner office picking his ear. You don't have to be a rocket scientist to figure that's the guy you want to be.

Me, I dream of beaches, palm trees waving in the wind. I gravitate to books about space travel and biographies of people who gave it all up for the South of France, say, or the South Sea Islands. In meetings, I find I can't listen to meaningless drivel anymore without feeling the urge to get up and leave. That's a significant liability. PowerPoint presentations in particular put me into a sleep so deep it involves drooling. I'm up every night at 3 AM wondering why I'm up every night at 3 AM. No matter how small the potential snafu or fubar situation, it rears up and seizes my imagination like a golem. I need some relief. I may need to retire.

But then there's the whole problem with actual retirement. It's for old people. There they are, wiggly wobblies in their dotages, even the ones strong enough to play three hours of tennis and pound down a big sirloin for lunch are all vagued-out and weird. All those healthy, fit men and women with suntans and golf clubs and white, toothy grins handcuffed to their spouses. Wowsers. Who are they? I see them in the places I eat. They're in the back by the potted plants. They're talking about mashies and niblicks and great lies on the fifteenth fairway. When you ask them what it's like to be retired, they talk about golf, and they talk about all the organized travel they are doing, and in my mind's eye the void opens up like a cosmic space that only Stephen Hawking could understand, a place where people mall-walk in fugue states. I'm scared to retire. That way lies senescence, superfluity, and too much thought about fiber. Not to mention, you know, Death.

Some middle ground is called for. Something between the grinding labor of working life and the quiet burble of the nap that precedes the long sleep. The good news is that I believe, after cogitating for some time on the subject, that I have discovered the answer: retire while you're still working. You don't have to be a big shot to pursue the dream. Anyone with a job and the desire to shirk it is eligible.

The superiority of "retirement" while employed over genuine retirement is evident:

| GENUINE RETIREMENT | "RETIREMENT" WHILE EMPLOYED |
| --- | --- |
| Fixed income | Big bucks with boffo bonuses |
| Lunch at Costco because it's the only place where you can get a giant hot dog and a Coke for $1.50 | Lunch at Michael's where you have a cheeseburger and Pellegrino for $150 |
| Small circle of acquaintances | Rich social context |
| Drink alone | Drink with "friends" |
| Drive 400 miles per year in boring personal car | President's Club at Hertz |
| Mandatory golf on same course, over and over, year after year | Elective golf on links around the world |
| Heart attack at price of T-bone | Take an extra one home for Rex |
| Lose touch with reality | Create own reality |
| Diminished sexual options | Possibility of still getting lucky now and then |
| Intimations of mortality | Estate planning |
| Too many naps | Precisely correct nap quotient |
| Wait too long for death | Occasional limited wait for limo |

Fortunately for those of us lucky enough to operate in this day and age, the contemporary business environment has provided us with the solution to this dichotomy. To gain the benefits of retirement while avoiding its pitfalls, one must simply learn how to live like an executive.

I invite anyone who doubts the utility of this strategy—which provides the underlying secret of executive life—to read the following brief clip, offered by Michael Lewis in the *Financial Week* of November 19, 2007. It concerns the now-ousted CEO of Merrill Lynch, Stan O'Neal, who in the preceding months had been facing the loss of billions upon billions of dollars in the subprime mess that year.

"In the six weeks between Aug. 12 and Sept. 30, as Merrill Lynch's losses mounted, its CEO didn't merely manage to play 20 rounds of golf, on four different courses. He played them beautifully, with a consistency that defied the pain he must have been feeling," Lewis writes, continuing:

> *Indeed, a glance at the scores explains why the Merrill Lynch board agreed to pay him $48 million in 2006: The man has ice water in his veins. From the end of July to early October, when the firm Stan O'Neal ran was losing money at a rate of more than $100 million a day, his handicap wavered only slightly—in fact dropped, to 9.1 from 10.2.*

It's hard to tell now if Lewis is kidding. But he goes on to quote what he contends are the actual notes O'Neal scribbled on the back of his PGA scorecards during the bucolic time he spent on the greens while his firm was bleeding red. "Many of these, naturally, have nothing to do with business," Lewis writes.

> *For instance, on Aug. 31 on the back of the card that proves he shot an 83 at Martha's Vineyard's prestigious Vineyard Golf Club, Mr. O'Neal scribbled, "Stan is certainly the man!" On Sept. 22, after he'd shot an 80 at the verdant Waccabuc Country Club, he wrote, with his natural ear for the language, "Eighty makes me greaty!"*

What's interesting to us in this exercise is not how egregious all of this is, but how enviable. Wouldn't you like to be playing golf, or something even more worthwhile, at a time when others are burning the midnight flopsweat? I know I would.

Cute, huh? I think so. Turns out that just weeks later, for some reason, O'Neal was gone from the firm. Those who are concerned about him will be relieved to know that he left with about $150 million in severance in his pocket. I expect him to have surfaced again by the time this book is in print, possibly at my company in some altitudinous capacity. Hell, I'll probably be working for him. Self-reinvention, built on the amnesia inherent in the system, is the hallmark of true executive talent.

The good news is that this charmed life of indolence and financial security is now within reach of us all. The key, I believe, is to use the digital capabilities, global reach, and evolved status of the delegative arts to build a lifestyle for ourselves that, if executed with distinction, replicates the faux retirement of the rich and infamous. At the heart of this strategy lies a phalanx of ploys, evasions, ruses, hoaxes, sleights of hand, and clever swindles that, from this time forth, we will bundle under one simple name: executricks.

These are the widgets, gadgets, and assorted tools that make a fun, lucrative working retirement possible. You can learn them too. Why not? If not you, who? And if not right now, when?

INTRODUCTION

# Core Concepts

For the executrick to take place at all, let alone work, it must first have soil to grow in, air to breathe, the environment and the necessary local technology to give it form and shape. If you toil in a culture without widespread use of the BlackBerry, for instance, or some other form of remote communication, you will have to essentially hop around on one leg to get things done. They can be accomplished, of course. But it's a lot harder. An apple pie made out of Ritz crackers is possible, for instance. It's called a Mock Apple Pie, and if you have no apples, that might have to do. It's better, however, to have apples.

Whether you have the optimal equipment or not, you must be clever. And wise. And around long enough to establish a working milieu in which you can rely on the following pillars upon which your temple of subtle, varied executricks will be built.

▶ Delegation. This is the art of getting other people to do the stuff you don't want to. It is at the heart of all power. You can't woolgather if you're the one responsible for shearing the sheep.

Great delegators of the past include both managers recognized for their wisdom and success and others noted throughout history for their indolence and stupidity. You can choose which one you'd like to emulate. History has a way of changing its mind about great delegators, and contrariwise those who don't delegate enough.

Ronald Reagan was widely derided at the end of his career as president for sleeping during meetings and allowing his wife to act as the actual chief executive, stomping on subordinates and otherwise setting the agenda in matters of policy and astrology. At the same time, there were fawning exclamations of devotion from places usually as circumspect as the dean of business publications, *Fortune* magazine, which ran a famous story entitled "What Managers Can Learn from Manager Reagan." Today, a huge number of Americans cite Reagan as one of the great presidents in American history, with nary a word implying that the man snoozed through a fair amount of his second term.

The operational implications are very clear. Those who can establish a style of delegation are well on the way to setting up the comprehensive environment in which the executrick can function. There will be no retribution, either in real time or the future, if the shifting of responsibility is seen as a bona fide and

## CORE EXECUTRICK:
### *Delegation*

1. Receive work;

2. Designate recipient;

3. Assign work;

4. Monitor as necessary;

5. Receive work;

6. Evaluate and redelegate;

7. Receive revised work;

8. Accept work with thanks;

9. Pass along work to original source; accept credit;

10. Continue policy of inattention.

elected tactic. Only those who take on the job and then simply fail to perform will find trouble. The core executrick is to pass along the work and then make certain that the recipient of the assignment accomplishes his or her task and then passes along some portion of credit to you. Along with this modus vivendi comes the danger that your working retirement will be interrupted rudely if your designated hitters screw up. Stan O'Neal felt groovy on the golf course because he thought the guys back in the office could handle things. Now he has to go home with nothing but $146 million to fall back on. Sad story, huh?

Artful, crafty delegation is the foundation of our craft. Without it, nothing can rise. But it is only one of the concepts that drive the enterprise, primarily by empowering the next core element of our effort:

▶ Absence, or the ability to get "work" done while not being physically on the scene.

We will spend quite a bit of time exploring the many possibilities here, which, in this digital age, are abundant and quite nuanced. But the underlying principle has been in play since

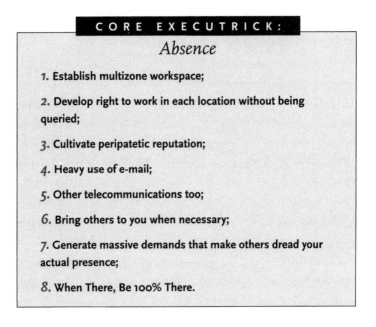

**CORE EXECUTRICK:**

*Absence*

1. Establish multizone workspace;

2. Develop right to work in each location without being queried;

3. Cultivate peripatetic reputation;

4. Heavy use of e-mail;

5. Other telecommunications too;

6. Bring others to you when necessary;

7. Generate massive demands that make others dread your actual presence;

8. When There, Be 100% There.

ancient times, when great rulers like Alexander and Caesar ran the known world from Illyria, Thrace, Macedonia, and other remote places from whence there was no public transportation. News took weeks to get anywhere, and then arrived garbled. And yet they somehow made the state of Not Being There work for them on a very high level. And believe you me, they both had a mighty good time while doing so.

Today, great potentates from Putin to Gates are honored more in the breach than the observance most of the time. These are executives who have mastered the ability to be perceived as working even when they are, in effect, invisible. Can you imagine anybody in the Kremlin gassing on about how lame the boss is, even though he hasn't been seen in the Pedestrian Control Department for years? No. That's because Putin is totally there, even when he's not.

On a much lower level, there's the average business manager who must establish a similar level of bogus presence in order to pursue his or her working retirement. Most of us don't have the power of a Howard Hughes, who became a potent fictional, even mythical, force well before his own actual physical existence became unnecessary. Still, approximations abound. I have certainly known executives who spent more time in Africa with Bono than they did with their reportees at boring old corporate headquarters, and were still obeyed and well loved.

That's because active, engaged absence has never been easier. We have cell phones and personal digital assistants that can bring us information or deliver orders anywhere in the world. I was out in Hawaii recently, at an utterly remote place that could be reached only by a one-lane road that snaked along the edge of a terrifying jungle precipice. Sure enough, my BlackBerry was at full four-bar power. I was so annoyingly accessible I had to put the stupid thing in a drawer to attain any peace. Across the globe, the climate, altitude or terrain notwithstanding, groves of ugly, fake, spiky evergreens are sprouting up, even as we speak, each of them in actuality a powerful cell tower. The bright side of this is that it is verifiably true that at this stage of the game nobody really needs to be anywhere, let alone somewhere, because everybody is, in a sense, everywhere.

If you can wrap your mind around that, you're ready for the next, slightly more intricate concept.

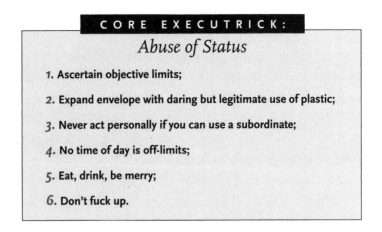

## CORE EXECUTRICK:
### *Abuse of Status*

1. Ascertain objective limits;

2. Expand envelope with daring but legitimate use of plastic;

3. Never act personally if you can use a subordinate;

4. No time of day is off-limits;

5. Eat, drink, be merry;

6. Don't fuck up.

▶ Abuse of status, primarily via the creative utilization of plastic.

Perhaps I've put that a bit harshly. Warren Zevon said it best, I think. When asked, at the end of his life, if he had any advice for those who wished to make the most of theirs, he replied, "Enjoy every sandwich."

When cast in a business setting, a host of possibilities assert themselves. How many sandwiches there are to be enjoyed! All of them legitimate! Many of them with caviar inside, sitting proudly on the buffet area of the corporate G4! The mind boggles.

One must be adroit, it goes without saying. I have in mind the cretinous numbskulls who dined on their company plastic a couple of years back, I think it was in Paris. They were lawyers from an American firm, putting their expenses on the client, I believe. Anyhow, in an evening that has become an urban legend, these guys ordered, like, $50,000 worth of wine at dinner. They had to pay it all back, naturally. Perhaps they even lost their jobs, I don't know. The reason I don't know is that, as egregious as their behavior was, I can't seem to find a single thing about it on Google. Think of all the minuscule, inconsequential niblits you can find on Google. Not this. These guys screwed up big-time. And what they did is NOT remembered. Think on that for a little while.

The goal, however, is to not be a short-term dork. A life in business may be well spent when nothing personal is spent at all. This freedom to expand and breathe within one's income is a vast improvement on the economic status of genuine retirees, even those worth billions. Actually, it may be true that the more money one has, the less one likes to spend it. I know one supergazillionaire who always takes the contents of the sideboard home at the end of a catered business meeting. Another steams stamps off envelopes and reglues them for future use. This psychotic level of frugality in the very rich may explain why many who could actually chuck it all and enjoy their hard-earned gold during their golden years are now sticking around instead. True retirement stinks. What we're talking about here is actually much better. As important as wealth is, it needs to be augmented by a certain kind of status, a position conferred by one's place in the world, a sense of importance in the vast scheme of things that has nothing to do with the money.

When I say that, I want you to take me at my word. Very often, when people say, "It's not about the money," they are lying. In fact, most people who say, "It's not about the money," actually mean, "I'm embarrassed to tell you that it's about the money. So I'm not going to. But it is, or I wouldn't say it's not."

In this case, however, it's really not. Status is also about where they put you at Spago or Michael's or The Palm or The Four Seasons or the Ivy or Mortons or IHOP or Denny's, depending on your sphere of operations. It's about your seat at the boardroom table. It's about the looks you get when you enter a room. You can't quantify that. But the genuine false retirement requires the absolute maximization of this factor, because most of the time you are actively playing the role of a functional entity. You can't win if you don't play. And part of being a player is all about getting your props and looking the part.

It's not all about appearances, however. In order to generate the right to appear important, businesspeople of any size or power at all have mastered the art of appearing decisive when they have no idea what's going on. This inevitably requires the ability to arrive at credible decisions quickly and virtually without thinking, and to somehow convince others that they haven't handed the car keys over to an idiot.

This delivers us to the next core concept, as the successful working retiree demonstrates the ability to be:

▶ Decisive, even when confused.

---

**CORE EXECUTRICK:**

## *Decisive When Confused*

*1.* **Listen to issue;**

*2.* **Take appropriate time to "think about it";**

*3.* **Target key alternate worker;**

*4.* **Transmit decisiveness;**

*5.* **Remain on e-mail chain!**

*6.* **Get lost.**

---

This is a very difficult executrick for those who have yet to fully embrace the lifestyle of the rich and fatuous. We are trained to approach decision making in a certain responsible manner. The seasoned executive seeking surcease from daily sorrows, however, must relearn that process. The key is to move dynamically and without fear to create work for others that will engage them while you are doing things more to your liking. While they are meeting, researching, constructing documents for further review, you will of course be somewhere else, managing, presumably.

In this regard, the seasoned executive will have on hand an agent of some sort who will pursue the agenda without hassling him too much about it for a while. This could be a subordinate, if you have any. Even an ambitious, willing peer will do.*

Believe it or not, there are also many, many senior types who haven't gotten the reality of the situation yet and are sweating for more to do. They are operating under the misapprehension that real executives look busy. The fact is, the really powerful mogul types look more like Donald Trump. Have you ever seen him look busy? He always looks cool, confident about his hair (for no discernible reason), and about to take his wife dancing after purchasing her an ostentatious new necklace. Sweat? Not he. The only time you see him exercised about

---

* This may be referred to as the "whitewash the fence" scenario taken directly from Twain. I would explain it to you but that would be more work than I intend to do in this footnote. Ask somebody. Or better yet, look it up online. The Internet is now one of the chief tools for those who, like us, seek to appear knowledgeable while in fact knowing virtually nothing. It's a godsend, actually.

anything is when he's taking a swipe at somebody who got on his nerves in the media.*

How about Warren Buffett? He looks like he just had a turkey dinner and is on his way to read a good book written by one of his friends in the financial sector, or take a nap, which is pretty much the same thing. Steve Jobs appears always to have just returned from a spiritual awakening at his remote ashram on the top of a Tibetan mountain.

The vice president of something down the hall, however, is another story entirely. He's only too eager to dine from your plateful of to-dos. Very often, if you can be decisive and bossy in his face, you can deflect a huge amount of work-related debris away from yourself and into this willing receptacle. All it takes is the talent of seeming certain when you are not, and imparting that confidence of what to do to somebody willing to do it.

As we veer toward this arena, where some form of activity is actually called for, we find the final core concept. It would seem to be something of a departure from our agenda, but really isn't. We have no need for it except in genuine times of crisis, but then it is truly essential:

▶ Intense engagement.

This is going to break your heart, but a little reality check never hurt anybody. Here it is: you aren't really retired. Not yet. You are still on the company's teat. You must still show up at

---

* Which is why we like him so much!

> ## CORE EXECUTRICK:
> ### *Intense Engagement*
>
> 1. Perceive "code red" requirement for actual WORK;
>
> 2. Work very hard, in order to make work go away;
>
> 3. Have as much fun as possible while doing so;
>
> 4. Take the rest of the month off.

times when you'd rather not. You must, in short, still work, not "work," when it is necessary. This should not, in your mind, spoil your retirement. It should, in fact, enhance its precious special nature. Look how much of your time you have now to live like a wealthy pensioner! Is it too much to ask that, when certain conditions coalesce, you put the hammer down?

If you're going to have the license to kill, you have to kill occasionally. This is where you prove that you are still nonfungible and your contribution is necessary to the well-being of the enterprise. The executrick is to make this phase of your operation as brief, intense, and efficient as a heart attack.

Dangers abound here. You could get involved in the day-to-day press of work again and blow the whole deal. Or you could become embroiled in ancillary activities that gum up the retirement—committees, meetings, prep for future meetings, meetings about meetings that will prep future meetings—or you could get sucked up into a vortex of praise or blame that drains you of your will to relax. You could become angry or vengeful, or just the opposite, filled with the milk of human kindness and so unable to use other people for your executive needs. These are only some of the risks that must be conquered if our entire castle is not to fall into the sea.

Fortunately, we have our executricks. Like any other business activity, they take practice and commitment. But ah, the prize at the end of the quest! The blossoming tree of sweet little gumdrops you now have at your disposal!

What follows, built on these five core concepts, is a tasty buffet of executricks to help nourish you on your way to an active, working retirement. You may eat them yourself, savor them, use them to make your life easier. You may hurl them at other people in anger, or share them in friendship. Together, they will sustain you while you hang around earning money for as long as you like, basking like a happy little walrus on a beach of relative indolence.

It is executive life at the highest level, and it is within your reach.

# Executricks

On November 30 the Nagoya District Court accepted Hiroko Uchino's claim that her husband, Kenichi, a third-generation Toyota employee, was a victim of karoshi when he died in 2002 at the age of 30. He collapsed at 4 am at work, having put in more than 80 hours of overtime each month for six months before his death. "The moment when I am happiest is when I can sleep," Mr Uchino told his wife the week of his death. He left two children, aged one and three. As a manager of quality control, Mr Uchino was constantly training workers, attending meetings and writing reports when not on the production line. Toyota treated almost all that time as voluntary and unpaid.

THE ECONOMIST
DECEMBER 19, 2007

Far from idleness being the root of all evil, it is rather the only true good.

SØREN KIERKEGAARD

# I

## The Office, and the
## Manipulation of Space/Time

*A man's office is his or her castle.*
*SIR EDWARD COKE (1552–1634)*
*(UPDATED)*

*Hm?! Oh, my. I must have fallen asleep again. Happens to me just about every day at this hour, doesn't it. So nice to be able just to sack out on the couch whenever I feel like it. Nobody bothering me. No bells ringing, at least none I have to answer. I think I'll go downstairs and get myself a cup of cappuccino, extra foam, with a double shot of Colombian. And a cookie. Yeah, definitely a cookie. Better still, I'll have Doris do it. After that, I think I'll go online for a little while. Watch what's new on YouTube. Do some e-mail. Better not forget to water my plants. Better still, I'll have Doris do it. I wonder what time my next meeting is? I don't feel much like seeing anybody. I know. I'll have Fred do it.*

No, the person speaking above is not retired. The person we will be hearing from at the top of every chapter of this book is in the blessed state to which we aspire. He or she is an executive. And if we work very hard at not working very hard, we can live like executives too.

We have already explored in brief the five core concepts from which all subsequent executricks extrude. None may be utilized with distinction, however, unless we have a home turf, a base of action, a Fortress of Solitude to which we may repair when tired, bored, resentful, confused, angry, or simply out of ideas. In this chapter, we will be looking at how to create this blessed professional habitat.

This may seem rudimentary to some who have good office space already. To those who do not, the establishment of a fine and private place may seem an impossibility. Yet our program would be lame indeed if it served only those who were already in good shape. We must consider how to serve luxe and schmucks alike.

The first consideration is comfort. No executive can operate without a central commitment to personal well-being.

What are the elements of such physical ease? I would submit to you that, in a business context, the base requirement is a chair, one that is right for you. It could be a recliner made of fine Corinthian leather or a big blue ball on a tripod, it doesn't matter. Your chair is the place where you plant your base. From that, we may move on to other equally important objects and environmental entities.

It is possible that where you are right now in your career, you already have suitable seating. It is, however, unlikely. You could surely do better. Somewhere within the organization, possibly near you, there is someone with seating that would be more appropriate for you. You should probably go out and take it. In seizing that which you require and desire for yourself, you are taking one of the first steps toward being the kind of executive who may graduate to all kinds of cool stuff associated with the kind of ersatz retirement we're contemplating.

To put it another way, if you can't get yourself a chair you probably should quit right now.

I've been in the same chair since the time I was a junior associate in the department. That's because from the start my chair was perfect for me, for anatomical reasons it is unnecessary to enumerate. Without it, I would have had the sensation from the start that I was in somebody else's chair, somebody else's office, somebody else's career, somebody else's life. Eventually, I would have had a choice: to be somebody else, or to give my entire situation to that person, whoever he or she might be. Instead, I found the right chair. You should too.

Options in this regard include:

▶ Going through Office Services to order the chair you require;

▶ Waiting for the right chair to magically appear and then having the presumption simply to grab it and hold on to it;

▶ Finding a chair belonging to a weaker life-form and then taking it surreptitiously;

▶ Finding an unoccupied office with a suitable chair in it and making do with that.

I opted for the second alternative, which is not as dynamic as some but then again I'm never going to be the kind of psycho destined to be the chairman. I'm just normally duplicitous and selfish, which has served me well and probably will work for you too.

At the time, I was an associate-level droid seated in a tweedy thing with a floating back panel that made me want to lie flat on the floor after fifteen minutes of use. It was clear to me that others were more comfortable in their seats and that I would have to do something about the matter. There were several vice presidents who had what I wanted, but obviously I couldn't simply stroll in and wheel out one of their recliners.

So I waited for Ralph Hamilton, a clearly doomed individual

### EXECUTRICK:
## *Acquire Appropriate Seating*
### *(Active Scenario)*

*1.* Ascertain "dream chair";

*2.* Find location of existing chair within confines of office space belonging to nonlethal individual;

*3.* Wait until night;

*4.* Acquire possession of chair;

*5.* Transport to personal space;

*6.* If questioned, deny with outrage;

*7.* Enjoy chair as first evidence of executive potential and status.

from a prior iteration of senior management, to be fired in one of the regular end-of-year cutbacks that all corporations endure. The moment Chuck was gone, I swooped in and took his chair. There were others waiting in line for it, but once I had it, it would have taken (1) a really senior person to come in and lay claim to it, an unlikely event since most senior people already had their own special seating, or (2) a person on my level to challenge me straight-up for it. This was even more unlikely, because in organizational life very few people will ever challenge you straight-up about anything.

Obviously, the details of the bureaucracy in your locale may militate for a different plan of attack for the seizure of this treasured object. But all bureaucracies are subject to personal/professional influence if you find the right pressure point and have magnitudinous patience. If you are destined to be the kind of executive who patiently waits around and plays by all the rules of nicety, so be it. You're going to have a much slower and more deliberate road to retirement on the job. The most successful and powerful people in business tend to be the ones who just take the chair they want, even if it means killing the guy currently sitting in it.

Okay, then. We've got our comfy seat and now we're prepared to advance to the next phase of the first part of the initial portion of our inaugural effort. The muscles and stamina we built up getting our chair will not be in vain, because the next move is even more difficult, unless you are fortunate enough to have this crucial entity already.

## Acquire Appropriate Seating
### (Bureaucratic Scenario)

1. Shop with approved vendor online for "dream chair";

2. Contact internal department responsible for acquisition of chair, ascertain proper procedure, and individual responsible for decision;

3. Take that person to lunch, drinks;

4. Wait. Do favors for person;

5. Wheedle, wheedle, wheedle;

6. Wait some more. Prove executive stick-to-itiveness. Never give up;

7. Get chair; celebrate with drinks.

It's called a door. Virginia Woolf, the novelist and center of the group of sex maniacs called the Bloomsbury Group in the mid-twentieth century, perhaps said it best, contending that "a woman must have money and a room of her own if she is to write fiction." While many of us are not women and do not write or even read much fiction, her point remains a strong one. Very little that is creative and personally fulfilling can be accomplished if one does not have a quiet space that can be sequestered. And that requires a door.

To function at the bogus executive status to which we aspire, one must:

▶ Get a door or, if you are a Hobbit, some means of differentiating and defending your personal space;

▶ Maintain the integrity of your doorway;

▶ Establish the legitimacy of your right to close your door;

▶ Close your door with regularity and impunity.

There is, however, a totalitarian trend in contemporary workplace life—the cubicle. Cubicles are anathema to our pursuit of a dignified and productive retirement. If you are in a cubicle when you work, it is possible that you may still play the game, but you are like a horse that can count to ten at a convention of genuine mathematicians.

If you do work in a cubicle farm, however, believe me there are certain tricks that senior officers pull in order to give themselves privacy and room to play with themselves. Perhaps they have "thinking spaces" where, if they are in them, nobody else will venture. Maybe they take walks, or have a place in the basement where they go to play Halo, or a washroom with a lock on it. I don't know. Believe me, Sergey Brin doesn't do his thinking while sitting in the middle of a bunch of jabbering wonks.

## If You Are in a Cubicle

1. Angle your screen AWAY from the entryway, so that you can play games and surf the Web;

2. Get plants, posters, statues, trophies, anything that can personalize your space and make it uncongenial for others to be in it;

3. Cultivate patterns of unfriendliness that dissuade others from entering your sanctum; executives are often mercurial and assert the right to be unapproachable; this will create a virtual "door" between you and people who might otherwise invade your privacy. It also marks you as somewhat antisocial and difficult to deal with, i.e., executive.

Michael Bloomberg has a place he goes to when being a politician and big-time capitalist gets on his nerves and he can't stand to see the acres of cubicled slaves he has working for him. Study what the bosses do, and figure out your own way of emulating their charming ways.

But make no mistake: no privacy, no genuine fake retirement. All I can tell you is that without the ability to close yourself off you will not be able to:

▶ Nap;

▶ Woolgather/daydream;

▶ Go on YouTube/Play Tetris/Follow Thompson ticker;

▶ Have sex with yourself/others;

▶ Eat a big, sloppy sandwich without grossing others out, and diminishing their perception of you;

▶ Other.

Believe me, all of these are things that executives do, and if they can't do them they quit and go someplace they can. And all of these things depend on a door, either a physical door or a metaphysical one.

## EXECUTRICK:
### *Acquiring a Door*

*1.* Figure out what level of executive rates a door in your organization;

*2.* Get promoted to that level, or just below it;

*3.* When you are in hailing distance of having the right to a door, start whining about one;

*4.* Be enterprising and imaginative! Perhaps there is a closet without a window that nobody wants?

*5.* It's amazing how a stated objective often is Step One in getting what you want. Make your desires known! It's easy and fun!

There are many ploys you can employ to get that all-important doorway to the next level of the Massive Multiplayer Online Role-Playing Game we're engaged in. They all radiate from your ability to bend others to your will, either by storm or by a protracted campaign of wheedling and negotiation. Once again, these are the kinds of things that executives do. If you can do them too, you're one of them. If not? You may need to grow a pair in order to proceed.

Once you have the portal to privacy, you're going to need to set up the expectation that it will be closed at times for purposes both legitimate and mysterious. A door that must remain open is like a bottle of fine wine that may never be tasted, a gorgeous summer home that one is always too busy to visit. Like all executricks, this one is based on moxie, determination, and charm, qualities that must be acquired as we move along if you do not already possess them.

Since you are entering this MMORPG as a newbie, without the skills possessed by the murderous virtual entities with whom you must coexist, every trick you master makes you stronger, more fit to play. At first, each may seem impossible. You may die a few times while trying to build up your stamina or strength. But in the end, you will triumph, Zoltor!

We almost have our home base settled, even you who labor in the fascist cubicle salt mines. There is one more seemingly implausible thing you should work like the devil to make a part of your life.

Everybody needs an assistant. Even assistants need an

## *Establishing Your Right to Close Your Door*

*1.* From the moment you have a door, close it at certain regular times of the day;

*2.* At the outset, keep those periods of closure brief;

*3.* Attempt to mirror status of senior officer, then move outward to establish your own pattern;

*4.* Carefully expand time of closure, making sure to be alert while doing so, entering and exiting with some energy to show that closure is result of intense concentration, not simple goofing off;

*5.* Music/TV is helpful. If others become annoyed with sounds emanating from your office, it will be easier to be "considerate" and close yourself off;

*6.* If challenged, become truculent;

*7.* Primary rationale should always be increased productivity, but do not be shy about saying things like, "I was taking a nap, what do you think I was doing?" since all executives nap and will recognize a fellow spirit if you do;

*8.* Under no circumstances abandon your ongoing efforts. Eventually, you will win.

assistant. The idea of pursuing your retirement without one is daunting indeed. We're not talking about people who work for you in a designated function related to their job description. Let's hope you have one of those as well. We're positing the existence of somebody to do all the things that interfere with your effort to live as a plump, bloated, lazy, self-obsessed remora on the body of corporate life.

Things an assistant does for you:

▶ Scheduling, including not only setting up stuff but also canceling, with suitable excuses, events that you no longer care to attend or duties to perform when the time has come. Not doing things you don't care to do is the cornerstone of our enterprise;

▶ Reservations, most importantly for restaurants, which, if well done, establish 73 percent of your ongoing credibility as an operator;

▶ Travel arrangements, a totally time-consuming pain in the butt for any self-respecting business executive;

▶ Expense reports, an odious task that saps one's will to live;

▶ Answering the telephone, thus erecting a barrier to unpleasant interfaces. How many of those are there? More to the point, how many people does an executive really want to speak with at any given time? Three? On the other side, how many ex-spouses, importunate vendors, former associates who have been put out to pasture, needy subordinates are out there? A million?

▶ Pays bills, fills in papers/forms, etc. Ugh!

▶ Goes to drugstore, dry cleaners. No, it's not his/her job, but he/she is happy to do it anyhow, right? Sure!

▶ Gets lunch, because, you know, we're too *busy*.

▶ Like that.

Those of you who already have an assistant recognize that the existence of this person, like that of a suitable chair or a closable door, makes much else possible. Of course, good individuals are difficult to find and sometimes hard to keep, and bad ones are pandemic. I have been lucky during my servitude to be graced with quite a few of the former and, when I think about it, only one spectacularly horrendous specimen. I hasten to add that she was an exceedingly nice and well-meaning person, and she nearly destroyed my career.

Among other things, Marie Claire whittled away at my credibility and sanity by:

▶ Double-booking me in two places for lunch with some regularity;

▶ "Forgetting" about phone, BlackBerry, and Corporate AmEx bills and stuffing them all into a drawer for nearly two years until my credit rating was destroyed and I lost my plastic. Do you have any idea how much of my life is tied up with my plastic? But I digress . . .

▶ Telling me I was departing from Kennedy Airport when I was in fact booked out of Newark, making it necessary for me to get into a cab and pay, like, $100 to get to New Jersey from Long Island, then missing the plane;

▶ Things of that nature too innumerable and aggravating not only to mention but to conjure out of my memory.

The effect on my professional life was dramatic:

## Career Vector as a Function of Assistant

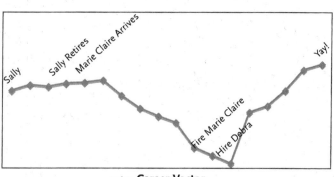

—◆— **Career Vector**

There are a variety of concepts involved in hiring the right assistant and tending and maintaining that relationship. Many are not so much tricks in themselves as common sense, involving kindness, clarity of expectations, consistent rewards, that kind of thing. I expect you to know about such matters. If you do not, refer to other textbooks on the art of proper management. That's not what we're up to here.

## EXECUTRICK:
### *Glomming On to an Assistant*

1. Most departments have an assistant of one form or another. Your job is to very slowly trick him/her into performing certain functions for you without attracting the censure of any competing managers;

2. Select a legitimate duty that you will be doing in service of the individual to whom the assistant reports;

3. Begin fobbing off tiny portions of this duty to the assistant, only after clearing this use of the assistant's time with the boss;

4. Very gradually expand the nature of these activities until they include some minor personal things that will "free you up" to do the core job better;

5. Continue to incent/bribe assistant to ensure that no animosity is engendered;

6. Maintain "freeing up" rationale over time. You now have access to an assistant.

7. When this situation becomes untenable, militate for an assistant of your own. You clearly need one!

We're more interested in those of you who do not have assistants and who need an executrick to get one. Obviously, they're not just going to assign you a helpmeet because you are looking to retire while you're still working. You have to create a scenario by which it is in the boss's best interest to make sure your ongoing efforts are supported by one. In so doing, you will glom on to someone else's assistant up to the point where it's clear that you generate so much activity that, you know, it's really ridiculous that you don't have some support of your own. It may be necessary for you to lobby for this, but if you're really tricky you can establish such a level of work for your boss's assistant that he or she just gets sick of the whole deal and gets you a low-cost one to avoid screwing up the rhythm of his executive retirement.

There may at times be significant roadblocks to this stratagem. Chief among these is the assistant who is unapproachable because he or she has too much power and can fend off your parasitic advances with ease. These most often fall in the region of what philosopher Georg Wilhelm Friedrich Hegel would refer to as a master/slave relationship gone topsy-turvy, which happens more often than one might think.

In this case, the ostensible "servant" gains excessive power over the supposed "master," and although both terms are certainly objectionable in a business context, I'm sure you understand what I mean. How many executive assistants are there in your world who have over time assimilated the force and prerequisites of their bosses, to the point where people fear the assistant more than the executive himself? The assistant's power

## Rampaging Assistant Syndrome

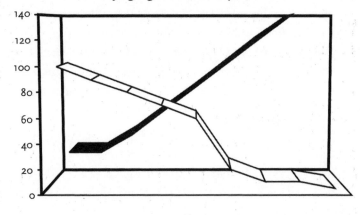

☐ Power of Boss  ■ Power of Assistant

grows, to some extent, in direct proportion to the increasing passivity and inattentiveness of the executive involved.

This is a clear downside of working for a manager who has retired while still on the job, because it makes the glomming process more difficult. You may have to search for a random weakling or powerless subordinate to fulfill the same purpose.

In the end—with your new chair, your establishment of privacy and the use, albeit limited, of another human being to assist you in virtually every aspect of your life—you are establishing a bubble. Like all bubbles, it has a membrane between inside and out. In our case, the membrane is made up of some of the things we have already discussed. It may also be composed of much more—limos, private jets, executive dining rooms. All will one day be yours, if you are tricky enough.

Within the bubble, there is peace and quiet, time moves in a certain stately manner, the air is clear and clean. Outside the periphery, all may be bedlam. But inside, life is as you need it to be, and you are free to move on to other helpful aspects of our ever-expanding agenda.

## 2

# Inhabiting the Electronic Void

*Nowhere man, the world is at your command.*
JOHN LENNON

*Gee, now what are these people babbling about? Oh yes, the first-quarter numbers. Blah blah blah. It's a good thing they haven't insisted on using the video teleconferencing capabilities for this weekly update or I'd have to get out of my underwear and I really don't feel like it. Who's that? Oh, right. Merganthaler, sucking up to Chet again. What a wanker. The sun is bright here in Santa Monica, even coming through the drawn blinds that way. I have to remember to put on the SP 40 when I go out later. God, I'm bored. I think I'll send a little BlackBerry message to Chet right now just to liven things up and make sure he knows I'm paying attention. "Hi, Chet," I'll say. "Can you believe what a blabbermouth Merganthaler is?" I know Chet checks his BlackBerry every couple of minutes. He'll see it and get a little chuckle and that will be nice. I like Chet. Maybe I'll drop back in at headquarters sometime soon. Better lose a bit of this tan first, though. Don't want people to think I'm doggin' it or something.*

———————

Just like the actual corporate marshals who have hung up their guns and badges, the working retiree doesn't need to be anywhere in particular. Unlike the true victim of perpetual leisure, however, the contemporary executive does have to give the appearance of gainful employment, and perhaps even do some "work," in order to perpetuate the game on a day-to-day basis.

We are indeed fortunate, therefore, to live in a time when electronics and digital technology have made the necessity for physical presence obsolete. In the world as we now know it, the person weighing in on an issue can be sitting right next to you or communicating via e-mail, BlackBerry, phone, or text message from 10,000 miles away while picking sand from between his or her toes. Depending on the executive involved, that can be either a grotesque or lovely image.

The other night, for instance, I was at a party in the northern part of California, a locale that has always been in the forefront of not working very hard while getting paid a lot for it. Back when there were still hippies, this took the form of lolling about, surfing, getting stoned on a variety of substances, and having transcendent experiences, physical, spiritual, and sexual, with a variety of whacked-out strangers. Now that people have settled down somewhat and have money, the lifestyle is more tame. People simply loll about, surf on water and Web, get stoned on a variety of substances, and coach peewee soccer, baseball, football, and volleyball, depending on the time of year and their level of dementia. They have less sex than they used to, but it's not for want of trying. In short, they are still living the dream.

I was standing next to a guy named Phil. We were both drinking an unpretentious Napa Zin with very big shoulders and a protuberant nose. People are very into wine in the area; in fact, it's one of the major topics of conversation business types turn to, along with real estate, the fate of the newest start-ups, and how the kids' teams are doing. After we exhausted those topics we still had at least four minutes left before either of us could move along without being impolite, so I decided to ask him what he did for a living, even though work-talk is generally considered somewhat outré in these parts.

"I'm the head of IT for a global solutions provider," he said. This surprised me. I had seen the guy three or four times at various gatherings, and he had always appeared totally smashed and given to waxing prolix on subjects that cannot be repeated in this august venue.

"Really," I said, trying not to appear surprised.

"Yeah," he said. "In fact, I'm working tomorrow."

This being Saturday night, I expressed some admiration at his industriousness, a quality I had not observed in great supply around these parts, except during the evenings of the middle school soccer draft.

"Yep," he continued. "I'm waking up at five AM tomorrow and going to Stinson Beach."

Stinson Beach is one of the remnant spots where people still have peyote with their cornflakes in the morning. "You work from there?" I asked.

"No," said Phil, looking at me as if I were stupid or something. "I surf there. It's nicely protected and the other surfers are pretty mellow, except for a couple of assholes. Water's cold as shit, though."

I was still waiting for the part where he would be working.

"Anyhow, it's no problem because I not only have the whole

rubber wetsuit but also when it's really freezing I have a hood that keeps me pretty much covered from head to foot."

I was still waiting for the part where he would be, you know . . . working?

"And I get there just as the sun is rising. It's really beautiful. And I sit in the parking lot with my laptop and my cell phone and BlackBerry. I get on any conference calls with London that I need to, and most of our offices in Asia are also up and running—those guys work pretty much twenty-four/seven and are totally in need of guidance, if you know what I'm talking about."

I must have offered a blank expression.

"They're very busy all the time but really disorganized," Phil continued. "Like, they want to work quite hard, actually, but have no idea what to be doing most of the time, so I've got to spend fifteen, twenty minutes with them every day to make sure they're not just running around like crazy chickens with their heads cut off. And then I go surfing."

"Don't you ever have to be in the office?" I asked him, my cheeks burning with excessive tannin and jealousy.

"Couple times a week," said Phil. "Just to see if my guys are doing what they're supposed to."

Get it? This guy is not a jerkoff. He's a boss. His firm books billions a year. And this is the way he does things. Do you think his reportees in San Francisco, San Jose, London, Dubai, Hong Kong, Tokyo, and Sydney see him in a wetsuit, sucking on a joint at dawn before plunging into the surf? I assure you they

## Using Your Digital Friends

*1.* **Cell phone:** Must be more important than your actual desktop telephone and be viewed as equally legitimate for business purposes;

*2.* **BlackBerry:** Total addiction necessary for those who wish digital independence; should have full calendar and address book capabilities;

*3.* **Laptop:** For development and transmission of substantial documents, so that one's location has absolutely no bearing on the dimension and importance of one's "work"; also peerless wireless Internet capability or it's a no-go, totally;

*4.* **Audio-Visual capability:** Suggested so that one need not be hauled in too often for teleconference calls;

*5.* **Other:** Be sensitive to new developments that may further enhance the power and viability of one's virtual existence.

don't. But he's getting the job done anyway. Most important, he is in the picture, so to speak, at every hour of every day, never far away, ultra-accessible, because the electronic nature of his job performance, rather than distancing him from his staff, actually makes him ubiquitous.

His manipulation of digital technology renders him terrifying, inescapable, and, as long as his department is functioning well, completely free of accountability for his whereabouts. He is, in short, a master executrickster, and a model for us all.

Now . . . how do we get there from here?

The key insight, I believe, is that the digital implements that have been invented so far, and those yet to come, are intended not to be supplements to everyday business activity, but to, in fact, supplant them as the primary conduits of orders, information, and "work." Going forward, face-to-face interaction will be necessary solely for interpersonal relationship building, which is not to be sneezed at but may be indulged in at your discretion.

All things being equal, it should be possible for an intelligent bot to do your job, except for the drinks after work with the Sales guys.

In order to institute the operational primacy of digital communications, you must first set up a new set of management expectations for yourself and the people who work with and for you. This is a gradual process. At no time should you set off any bells and whistles with your new way of getting things done. This could cause executive recoil from your modus operandi and cost you months if not years in the progress of our operation.

As you work on managing management, you must also produce excellent, consistent work product *in absentia*, utilizing the new tools of the trade. It also doesn't hurt to set up remote work locations where it's sort of expected you might be for some reason. I know a guy who set up a shop for his corporate function in Vegas and now people barely roll their eyeballs when he's there

## Managing Management Expectations in the New Digital Environment

1. In the beginning, *ask permission* to attend meetings of escalating importance in a digital format—speakerphone, teleconference, etc. After some time, this will become the expectation;

2. When you do so, always *be vague about where you are.* Your goal is to make this a nonissue;

3. Use e-mail to convey not only formal but private thoughts to senior management, being careful to cc: only appropriate parties. Provide value with each e-mail;

4. For some time, make sure the reason you are not in situ is that you are doing actual, nondigital work in the remote location; become viewed as a person who works hard anywhere or is "traveling";

5. Remain sensitive to management annoyance, but determined to establish a high level of invisible competence;

6. Keep your own people terrorized from afar.

in the middle of a New York winter. This is because he went whole hog on the project, selling senior management on the wisdom of the investment, and actually constructing a totally self-reliant, parallel operation that cost the corporation a lot of money. Now that expenditure needs to be justified. So he's there,

## Working the BlackBerry

1. Create your own BlackBerry tempo that rises and falls with the 24-hour biorhythm of your style;

2. Make sure all communications have a purpose;

3. Stay off inane chains;

4. Change your subject line!

5. Do NOT EVER "Reply All" without thinking once, twice, three times;

6. No profanity unless you are above the rank of Executive Vice President;

7. No jokes unless they are (1) funny and (2) not embarrassing if published;

8. Reply quickly to action items, slowly to thought-based items;

9. Use silence to sow confusion and communicate opprobrium.

valiant warrior, to do just that. They do good work out there, too. Important stuff. Of course he has to be there.

Let's take a look at each of the digital implements that you will need to master to get your road show on the road. All are essential and each must be used with craft and not abused as if it were a toy.

## Required Chargers

1. BlackBerry: Car/plane (2) and wall outlet for each work location and home;

2. Cell phone: Car/plane (2) and wall outlet (6) as well as one that ties into the laptop's USB port for maximum safety;

3. Laptop computer: Airplane jacks, two kinds depending on airline; wall outlet for hotel, home, and office (up to 8, since you never have one when you need one);

4. iGo "Swiss Army" charger with multiple interface jacks: Available at airport electronics stores;

5. Extra batteries for laptop, phone, etc.

First and of greatest importance is the BlackBerry, or whatever tool you use to message other people both inside and outside your corporation.

The BlackBerry is you. You are the BlackBerry. When people look at their BlackBerrys, they must see and feel your presence even when you are not there. If you do not create and preserve this constant presence that invades the lives of all who share your domain, your power and influence will molder. If, however, you come pouring down the digital pipe with consistency and force, the BlackBerry can be a tremendous tool for both personal freedom and control of others, including those who supposedly tell you what to do.

There are a host of tricks associated with this primary, essentially impersonal tool that carries with it so much personal power. Speed is important, as is strategic silence, which can make people absolutely crazy when employed correctly.

Most important is the concept of BlackBerry tempo. Everyone has his or her own that conveys the extent of their engagement/madness both in a general way and on any given subject. The following chart maps times of intense BlackBerry involvement in three separate executives—A, B, and C—by time of day.

## BlackBerry Activity 6 AM— 6 AM

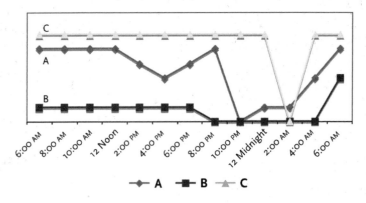

You may guess which ones are both the most successful as well as the least "present" in a physical sense throughout the working week. That's right. Executives A and C are both nuts and utilize the digital hardware to an extent that has paralyzed their everyday lives. Both make nine figures and are seen only in the company's orientation videos and occasionally at industry seminars held by investment banks. Executive B, who owns the relatively lowest-level presence on the chart and actually sleeps at night, works the hardest and is least addicted to the Black-Berry. He also makes the least money and is going nowhere.

A final word on the subject of this omnipresent fact of life in our mobile, peripatetic existences. There are, at present, a lot of jokes going around about people who are addicted to the "Crack-Berry." I'm sure there are those who find such jokes funny, the way people used to laugh at Cheech & Chong movies in the 1970s. But there is nothing amusing about true BlackBerry addiction. Be on the lookout for it in yourself and others, for it often presages the collapse of marriages, friendships, and wellness, not to mention the decay—and in severe cases, paralysis—of the ligaments between the thumb and forefinger.

Symptoms of last-stage addiction include:

▶ Incessant checking of the device when only moments have passed since the last such inspection;

▶ The sending of e-mails for no reason other than the need to do so, becomes overwhelming;

▶ Waking in the middle of the night and being unable NOT to look at the BlackBerry, and, in instances of true mental illness, to respond at that hour;

▶ The frenetic patting of various pockets in search of the device when it's not present;

▶ Phantom sensation of vibration when device is absent;

▶ Drooling, trembling, and insane gibbering when it is misplaced.

At this writing, there is no known cure for BlackBerry addiction and no support groups for those afflicted. The syndrome, like other addictions beneficial to the corporation (like workaholism), is not yet recognized as a genuine illness except by the loved ones of those affected. The only solution seems to be complete, cold-turkey reversion to in-person, analog existence and the abandonment of any hope for the form of extended executive retirement of which we dream.

So unless you are a true mogul with no hope of redemption as a human being, treat the thing with the same respect you would hard liquor or firearms. Give your BlackBerry a rest during weekends (at least six hours of daylight time) and put it in a drawer while on vacation (a shot in the morning is acceptable, but beyond that you need help).

The BlackBerry is, of course, only a medium, a delivery system. With all due respect to Marshall McLuhan, the message or messages carried on that system are discrete from the thing itself, and a vast region in which the executrick must function. I am speaking, of course, about the entity of e-mail itself.

Beginning as a trickle of electronic squiblets between computers several decades ago, e-mail has become the standard of all human communication, supplanting even the telephone among those who are too busy, self-involved, or emotionally inept to deal with other people.

Thus, superb use of electronic mail is absolutely essential if we are to proceed to the next level of our exalted, vacuous status.

There are precisely six general categories of e-mail communications that may be transmitted over computer, BlackBerry, or other handheld device. Each of these six is useful in its own way for the person seeking to avoid hard labor and convey maximum executive vagueness and clout.

Note that e-mail is also an excellent method of delegating labor-intensive activity privately, efficiently, and with no opportunity for whining and evasion from those who are being saddled with the task at hand.

E-mail should be a scalpel. A scalpel cuts. A scalpel separates tissue from bone with delicacy. But hit somebody over the head with one and they'll just look at you funny.

The form is meant to convey data and to promote function— primarily other people's function—and very little more. A perfect e-mail strategy, employing short, effective orders, admonitions and exhortations in real time, can be a better management technique than a welter of in-person blather. And less is more, particularly since most people are reading what you're writing on a tool with an itty-bitty screen.

Together, great e-mail technique and mastery of the Black-Berry almost get us to the nowhere status we seek. There

## The Six Forms of E-Mail

| TYPE | USAGE | EXAMPLE |
|------|-------|---------|
| The short e-mail | Approvals or denials | "Okay"/"No"/"See me" |
| The medium-sized e-mail | Discussion, with ass-kicking potential | "There are several things that disturb me about this. I'd like to know why this got so far without my input." |
| The long e-mail | To be delegated and then, when completed by others, returned to your mailbox and forwarded to senior officers under your byline | Long e-mails are for mid-level functionaries |
| The e-mail that's too hot | Kick-ass with extreme prejudice | "I suppose you think there's a rationale for this. I'd be very interested to hear it." |
| The e-mail that's too cold | Inserts icepick, leaving the target way too dead | "Proceed as you think best. You will anyway." |
| The e-mail that's just right | Gets business done, builds loyalty, delegates responsibility, diffuses blame | "Let's have a drink after work, Len, and talk about what we need to do next. Thx. Bob." |

remains only the cell phone and the laptop to complete our digital arsenal. I must admit to a certain bias here. I love my many laptops, but for me the mobile phone seems a tool most suited to idiots. Just walk around the streets of any city in the world and you will see people nattering on them to no particular good effect, some of them with little earpieces that make them look like psychotics babbling to themselves.

Nearly 80 percent of the content of all human cell phone conversations seems to be about where the caller is located, as in, "I'm at the corner of First and Second Avenue. I'll call you back when I get to Second and Third Avenue." Who cares? Why do people have to constantly inform other people of their whereabouts at this stage of human history? And what are the implications for us as a species? In certain cities around the world it is impossible to see any person actually walking down the street thinking his or her own thoughts. Don't we need thoughts? And if not, since when?

Don't get me wrong. If these were people pursuing our noble goal of a nonworking, company-funded, corporate state–supported retirement, I would totally get it. But such is not the case. These are people who can't stand to be alone with themselves in the dark, cold bosom of the cosmos and believe they need to fill their heads with emanations in order to span the moments between when they're in one place and then they're in another.

We're not empty-headed bozos. We're retired while working. We enjoy the sunshine and the feeling of being on our own, particularly in bright, hot places that serve little drinks with umbrellas in them, sometimes even before noon. We don't need to inform a variety of people of our block-by-block location. Wherever we go, there we are. And that's a beautiful thing.

The primary use of the cell phone, I believe, is to divert work. Using the implement, you may refer people away from you to several locations: first, to your assistant, who can deal with the content of the call in a businesslike fashion; next, to your BlackBerry, to which, if they're serious, they can send an actionable message, and finally, to somebody else, who can deal with whatever it is.

I have seen only one true world-class executive who seems to be wedded to his mobile phone for substantial reasons, and that

### EXECUTRICK:
## Containing the Cell Phone

*1.* Primary purpose: Provide executive assurance that you are reachable; no on-the-job retirement can be accomplished if that perception is not maintained;

*2.* Secondary purpose: Delegate responsibility; for many people this is easier to do when they are dealing with others remotely;

*3.* Tertiary purpose: Make dinner reservations, other social effluvia.

is Barry Diller, who appears to use it to scream at people on the way to lunch. He's doing well, so there may be a strategy to explore there. Time will tell.

With great BlackBerry technique supporting excellent e-mail skills and a proficient usage of wireless technology to transmit genuine work product from a decent laptop, the cell phone fades as a primary tool for the individual seeking nowhereness. In fact, the capacity of this implement to soften the brain may render it an actual detriment to human perfection, which until now has always been somewhat tied to the process of thinking in one form or another. We seem headed in the opposite direction:

## Cogitation in Cell-Phone Users

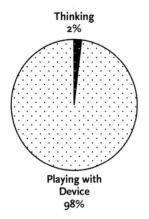

Thinking
2%

Playing with
Device
98%

If your alone-time looks like the pie chart on page 41, you may not be seeking retirement. You may be in search of an empty mental brain pan. Try Zen instead. It's been known to lead to a much higher level of enlightenment and comes with unlimited minutes.

# 3

## Meetings and
## the Technology of Everyday Life

*Monday nothing*
*Tuesday nothing*
*Wednesday and Thursday nothing*
*Friday for a change a little more nothing*
*Saturday and Sunday nothing*
THE FUGS

*Let's see now. My weekly calendar, printed out clean and neat from Outlook. Nothing Monday until 11, when I've got a meeting about a meeting we're going to be having in six weeks. Nothing of importance will happen about that meeting until the fifth meeting and this is only the third. I'll send Minkoff. That gives me a clear morning until noon. Not a bad start to the week. Three lunches—Tuesday, Thursday, and Friday. None too odious. I'm interested in that new Mediterranean place nearby. I hear their grilled octopus is out of this world. Staff meeting on Wednesday with all key people who report to Bob. I love those things. Sit around. Talk a little. Say hi to everybody. Have a danish. Two dinners. Poker Thursday night with the guys from Sales. Love to play with those guys. They always think their hands are better than they really are. A good week, all in all. Nothing lethal, no particular exposure on the downside. I think I'll get a rundown of all pending projects from Mortimer. Find out where we might fall behind on anything and torture my staff for a while. Weather's changing. Still pretty nice, though. Take a walk after lunch, maybe. First a little e-mail, make sure I know where all the bodies are buried. I wonder where the morning papers are. Doris!*

---

Mies van der Rohe, the great Bauhaus architect, believed that form follows function. It is he who said, "God is in the details," a statement so true and timeless that it has taken its place in the pantheon of great thoughts that seem to have been uttered by Anonymous. The notion is particularly relevant to our exercise. The function we are striving for is pure, simple, clean, and virtually eventless, the essence of retirement, with a little dash of excitement thrown in because, after all, we're not liver-spotted tortoises headed for the last beach yet, are we?

The function being pristine and devoid of filigree, the form of our days must be equally Spartan and Bauhausian, if that is indeed a word.

Think of your schedule, the granular makeup of your days, as, perhaps, the Lever House in New York City—clear, simple, all right-angled glass and steel. Everything that comprises it is necessary, nothing is for show. Every beam and window is necessary to hold up the structure. Anything extra has been jettisoned. And every piece of the edifice does its job exactly as it was designed to do.

The structure of your day is not formed of glass and steel, of course. Instead, it is made of meetings, interpersonal interactions, exchanges of paper, telephone calls with some putative content in them and those with none. Each must mirror the basic simplicity and elegance of your employed retirement.

The central issue to be dealt with first is the misapprehension of most middle managers that a busy schedule is the hallmark of a successful career. To some extent, of course, this is

## The Bauhaus Schedule

1. **Lean and easy:** While cramming the day full of stuff is sometimes unavoidable, it's not a good thing, a priori;

2. **Shapely:** A great day has a contour to it, and does not blow out of the gate like a wild bull; inescapable activity builds and then subsides;

3. **No filigree:** Except for the odd trip to the proctologist, retired people do not have portions of their day when they want to kill themselves because of something odious they have to do; get rid of those immediately unless they involve an unavoidable senior interface;

4. **White space:** There is time for thinking and, more important, nothing;

5. **Fun:** That's right.

true. In the first years of a job, one is building function. Very often, you're the repository of duties for a more senior officer who is well on his or her way to her own working retirement. Those are the years when activity from morning until night—and sometimes through the night—is not uncommon. At a certain point, however, the time comes to strip away all that is unnecessary and, in a sense, pay it forward to the next generation of chumps.

This takes some courage. It's actually quite scary to look at an "empty" day and not feel like a lazy douche. Breaking out of that mental harness is a critical step as we move forward to a life of sanctioned inactivity. But you must. Until you can do nothing and still feel worthy of a big fat paycheck, you are not an executive, and you will not live the life you yearn for. So suck it up and have the guts to get unbusy.

You think Warren Buffett sits around grinding through meeting after meeting after meeting every day? I don't. I think he sees who he wants to see and talks with who he wants to speak with and leaves everything that might be unpleasant for him to a host of other people who are honored to starch his shorts. Your goal, then, is to bend it like Buffett.

It's all about control. Slaves and sweaty bureaucrats do not control their time. Their bosses do, though. Don't you want to pretend you're one of those? The amazing fact is that if you pretend for long enough you will magically become one. I don't know why that is, but it's true. The corner offices of the world are filled by people who acted like they ran everything well before they did. And the cornerstone of that is a happy and selectively unproductive schedule that establishes a shapely day for you, day after day.

The charts below show two days. One of them is mine circa 1990. The other belongs to an unnamed executive who does not wish to divulge his name or whereabouts.

## Shape of Ugly Day, circa 1990
### Level of Activity, 6 AM to 6 AM

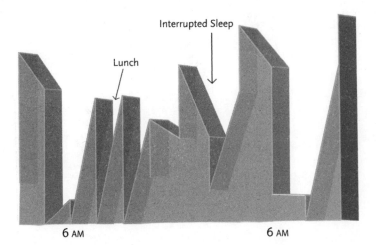

Interrupted Sleep

Lunch

6 AM            6 AM

The leftmost point of this horrendous workday begins at 6 AM with a phone call from some boss or other that immediately wrecks all plans and destroys any semblance of control for the rest of the day. As the twenty-four hours progress, constant inundations of effluvia boost activity to heart-attack levels, with incessant surprises, including some late at night, and only a few hours of troubled sleep. It is a life without elegance and, in some profound sense, intolerable.

Now let's look at the shape of an executive schedule, one that has been molded and crafted over time by an individual whose primary goal is to control his existence and not be a stressed-out, exhausted schlub for the rest of his life:

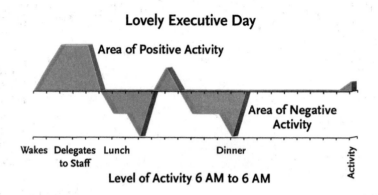

**Lovely Executive Day**

**Area of Positive Activity**

**Area of Negative Activity**

Wakes | Delegates to Staff | Lunch | Dinner | Activity

**Level of Activity 6 AM to 6 AM**

As you see, after a gentle awakening, there is a small spurt of activity in the mid-morning, as jobs are delegated and responsibilities moved to those who can do nothing to avoid them. There follows a relaxing morning followed by a pit of negative activity around noontime and into the mid-afternoon, when it is possible a nap is taken.* At about 4 PM, there is a final small spurt of engagement, possibly a conference call or a brief meeting on a not-unpleasant subject. There follows a long, enjoyable

---

* Negative activity may be defined as any pursuit that generates less than zero discernible work units. Included in this category are a variety of enterprises, including but not limited to sleeping, sucking on a mint, doing a crossword puzzle, instant messaging a social acquaintance, or looking out the window. The parameters of this concept are now being explored by customer service representatives at airlines, claims adjusters at insurance companies, and many others on the frontiers of sustained professional inactivity.

period preceding an attenuated stretch of complete somnolence. The tiny bump at the end of the range represents a short period of BlackBerry interaction upon wakening.

This kind of idyllic existence can be executed only by an individual in total command of the granular details of quotidian existence, and the executricks involved with each.

The meeting is the most disruptive element to any on-the-job retirement. It is a commonplace observation today, far more than it was, say, twenty years ago, that meetings are a drag on

---

**EXECUTRICK:**

## Core Assumptions on Meetings

1. No long meeting should take place if it can be replaced by a short meeting;

2. No short meeting should take place if it can be replaced by a phone conversation, e-mail, or memo;

3. Essential meetings should involve only those who are necessary to make decisions;

4. One need not attend meetings in which one's purpose at the meeting is either purely formal or wholly unclear;

5. It is the responsibility of every person at a meeting to get to closure as soon as possible;

6. The best possible meeting is the one that is actually a conversation between two people not afraid to make a decision.

---

productivity, a waste of time, and so forth. And yet we still have too many meetings about meetings, too many long ones, short ones, stupid ones, ones with too much content, not enough content, and so on and so forth and blah blah blah to the max. The problem is, meetings are like the weather. Everybody talks about them but nobody seems capable of doing anything about them.

It's simple. He or she who cannot control this issue can't assert the overall level of career control necessary to establish a working retirement. Certain core assumptions on the issue must be established if we are to impose some structure on the generally wayward nature of the phenomenon.

There are many, many types of meetings, each of which needs a different approach.

**The brief meeting (unplanned):** Often taking place in elevators, restrooms, or hallways, this is one of the prime ways that executives get out of stupid, time-wasting gatherings. This is also known since the 1980s as *managing by walking around,* a

---

### EXECUTRICK:

## The Brief Meeting
### (Unplanned)

1. Find an agenda point;

2. Ascertain agreement;

3. Make a decision;

4. Zip up and get out.

---

pompous name for what may accurately be described as trolling the office with a cup of coffee.

Keep on the lookout for such chances, and never, ever make the mistake of thinking that decisions and actions taken during such interfaces are not "real" meetings or are in some way nonbinding.

I was on the executive floor not long ago and I ran into Boorstein, a notoriously meeting-addicted dude. We had a piece of business to transact. We talked about the situation and came to an agreement about the way it should be handled. As I was preparing to depart, thinking to myself, "Well, there's another boring, useless meeting avoided," Boorstein says to me, "I'm glad we got our ducks in a row on this. It'll make our meeting on it later this week a whole lot easier." I almost said, "Ed, what the frig do we have to have another meeting on this for? We just handled it." But I figured, hey, Boorstein lives for the setting up, conducting, and backwash of continual meeting. "Sure, Ed," I said. And I sent Vreeland, my number three guy, to the meeting. I had other things to not do.

**The brief meeting (intentional):** There are other times when a quick, organized "drive-by" is necessary to get something done. These must be quick (five minutes, max) and definitive. The brief meeting is almost always made necessary by the need of a junior person to force a decision from a senior one. There are times when an executive in search of a nice nap will be forced to call his people together for a quick hit, but those must be kept brief, too, unless a certain amount of scratching and jiving seems appropriate.

## The Brief Meeting
### (Intentional)

1. Scheduled at short notice;

2. Aura of critical import;

3. Senior officer involved;

4. Get decision, then leave.

I don't mean to seem churlish or antisocial, and for many people the business meeting is the only socialization that they get. The goal, therefore, is not the elimination of such human intercourse, but rather the imposition of control on the situation. No control? No retirement. So drop by Mr. Beandip's lair when you feel like it, or set up a weekly gathering of all the guys you like to chew the fat and kick the hackeysack around with. But make sure it's you—or more to the point, your assistant—who's setting the terms in virtually all occasions, or you might as well just keep on working for a living until you and your aneurism enjoy that final date it's been planning for you.

**Long meetings:** The only ones of these that I enjoy are staff meetings, because they have a rich subtext. Friendships, alliances, mutual bonding, and discipline—all are featured in a good staff meeting. Everybody gets a little face time with Bob. People report on their best efforts. You see where the crevices

## The Staff Meeting—
## Make It Count

*1.* Come prepared with a very specific list of things you would like to report on;

*2.* Wait your turn patiently for the conch;

*3.* Be upbeat in your comments, but not stupidly optimistic. If business kinda sucks, say so;

*4.* If there is food, eat, but don't be the last one gobbling down that muffin;

*5.* You may ask questions, but unless you work with a bunch of buttholes, don't ask stuff that will humiliate your peers in front of Bob;

*6.* You may ask questions of Bob, but none that involve genuine content that he might not want to reveal in an open group;

*7.* Don't make jokes unless you are the appointed Fool and know what you're doing;

*8.* Afterward, hang around a bit and see who's interested in being your friend, and also who is interested in being the friend of your enemy.

might lie in the upcoming weeks and months. You hear about things. Unlike most meetings, gatherings of monkeys who hang together on the corporate tree are almost never a waste of time. They can go on a bit long, but that's a chance to BlackBerry your pals under the table to complain about Ferdlinger, who just doesn't know when to shut up.

There are many less congenial and interesting forms of longer meetings, including teleconferences, which occasionally must be endured and may even be fun if you're the one in the hot tub with Bambi while the rest of the guys are in the twenty-fourth floor conference room. If you are on the remote line, speak when spoken to or when you're supposed to be rendering value to the hideous enterprise, but not much more than that. If you do it right, people will even forget you're on but you'll still get credit in the big book of Life for being Johnny-on-the-spot even when you're on the road. They can't see you're blowing bubbles while they go through the out-year scenarios.

Then there are video teleconferences, which occasionally must be endured but are almost always a pain in the gonads. Nobody looks good on one of those video screens except perhaps at certain mega-ultra-hiphop-too-cool-for-school graphics and entertainment companies, who have built their twenty-second-century setups for global operations that pay millions and millions to keep everybody in touch so they don't have to spend a couple hundred grand to travel the right people to see each other. I have always thought that companies who are addicted to video conferencing are probably run by control freaks who can't stand anybody to be out of their sight. The experience always feels like prison to me, at any rate. It is prime delegation material.

I was at one of these companies in Los Angeles a few years ago.

## If You Are the Meeting Host

*1.* Be on time for your own meeting unless you are a jerk or are trying to piss people off;

*2.* Always have beverages at least, and if it's an hour where people might be hungry, have a little something to eat;

*3.* If there is nothing to eat, don't bring along your own cup of soup and slurp at it; I wouldn't mention it but you'd be amazed how many times I've seen an executive feed himself while everybody else starved;

*4.* Have an agenda and stick to it; exhort people to move along;

*5.* Offer good praise to those who deserve it, moderate any public blame you offer, even to those who deserve it;

*6.* Do not yell and scream, even if you feel like doing so; you may whine a bit if you must;

*7.* Do not talk on the cell phone while others are talking; how friggin' rude do you think your status allows you to be?

*8.* Unless it's some kind of merger thing or a team-building staff meeting, nothing over an hour. People have things to do. So do you, right? Sure!

You wouldn't believe their video conferencing studio. The entire wall was made up of HD flat-screen panels, the room linked up to similar setups in Europe, Asia, South America, and New York. You could sit in one city and the soul-patched, multipierced gang on Planet Mambo across the world would be right there in ultra-high-def right in front of you, life-sized. The call I saw was coming in from Amsterdam. You could almost smell the pot. That company had three projects that year. All of them bombed.

This is a book about getting out of work, not doing it, but it pays in this venue to talk about one very special subset of the lengthy meetings—the one at which you have to present—a PowerPoint presentation.

Make no mistake, ladies and gentlemen, PowerPoint is the greatest medium for bullshit ever invented. It makes even the most idiotic and badly thought out ideas look as cogent and strategic as any other. Like so:

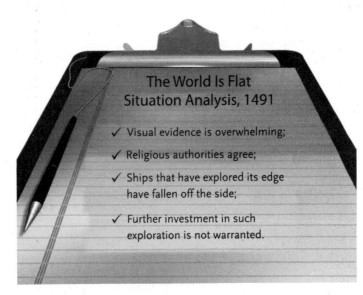

The World Is Flat
Situation Analysis, 1491

✓ Visual evidence is overwhelming;

✓ Religious authorities agree;

✓ Ships that have explored its edge
  have fallen off the side;

✓ Further investment in such
  exploration is not warranted.

This may be why PowerPoint is so popular with investment bankers trying to convince corporations to do flatulent things and new media people looking for venture capital to squander.

Worse, far worse, however, PowerPoint also is capable of taking good ideas and making them look shallow and vapid. Like this:

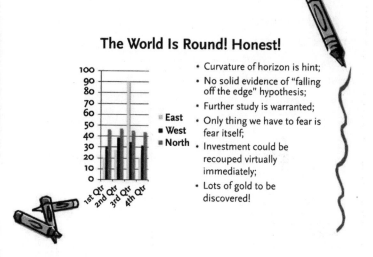

**The World Is Round! Honest!**

- Curvature of horizon is hint;
- No solid evidence of "falling off the edge" hypothesis;
- Further study is warranted;
- Only thing we have to fear is fear itself;
- Investment could be recouped virtually immediately;
- Lots of gold to be discovered!

See? Here is a perfectly good idea reduced to moronic vapidity, homogenized into pablum by the medium itself.

The bottom line is this: PowerPoint is bogus and people hate it. It bores them and fools no one into believing that anything of substance is behind it. Ninety-five percent of the time when the lights go down, people know they're in for a crock.

That does NOT mean, however, that this abused and over-used tool is of no use to you. It is my experience, and I may be going out on a limb here but I do think I'm right, that true masters of PowerPoint are so feared by people now that they are essentially unwelcome to the average resident of any meeting that has a hope of being effective, timely, and brief.

In other words, if you get a reputation for yourself as a big PowerPoint person, you may find yourself invited to fewer meetings and thanked profusely and dismissed once you have made your pitch.

In that regard, I would advise you to take PowerPoint very seriously and consider using it at certain key junctures when it looks like an issue might develop into a work-sponge. This does not mean, of course, that you want to give a bad show. You want your PowerPoint presentation to be accomplished and admired, while at the same time being despised enough to guarantee that you will rarely be invited to meetings. This creates something of a conundrum for those who actually want to do the right thing because they have, you know, some pride.

Ah, pride! It goeth before more meetings!

However, in the spirit of professionalism I will offer the two possible constructs you may employ in your career as a presenter. One will get you admired and sought after, and thus be retrograde to our efforts. The other will make you a legend as an expert and ensure that you have a lot of time to try that new place on Central Park South that has the $300 burger.

## PowerPoint Policy

| GOOD FOR THEM, BAD FOR YOU (CREATING MORE INVITATIONS) | BAD FOR THEM, GOOD FOR YOU (ELIMINATING INVITATIONS) |
|---|---|
| Brief in total length | No fewer than 50 charts, regardless of subject |
| Easy-to-read slides | Lots of tiny numbers and words on each |
| One overall theme | Tons of ridiculous digressions |
| No overbearing graphical elements | Cute pictures related to theme |
| Terse comments | Verbose expostulation |
| Occasional lighthearted chart | Lots of "funny" charts |
| Nothing personal | Rich with personal anecdote |
| Action points clear | Further study needed |

I assure you: Take the path on the left, and you will have plenty of meetings to go to for the rest of your life. Go with the right and you can phone in the remainder of your career from Bali.

# 4

# The Grand Meals
# of the Duc de Berry

*To everything there is a seasoning.*
*ECCLESIASTES*

*I love this place. In the morning, it's almost always invest-*
*ment bankers and other serious types, reading newspapers*
*and looking busy just like I look right now. But just because*
*I've got a copy of the* Wall Street Journal *in front of me*
*doesn't mean I'm thinking about bond futures. Ha. Right*
*now I'm thinking about those big fat rashers of bacon and*
*nice short stack of buttermilk pancakes that are on their*
*way. The best thing? Bissinger didn't show. Is there any*
*greater joy in this world than the moment you realize that*
*your breakfast companion isn't going to show up? Later on,*
*I'll start thinking about lunch. I hear the Core Club is good*
*for people who want to feel important about themselves, and*
*generally linger over their coffee and cookies. I think I'll take*
*Maureen Overby there. She's fun and almost never talks*
*business. Tonight, of course, I'm having that cowboy steak at*
*Porterhouse with Larry, Murray, and Ed. I wonder which of*
*us will pick up the check? My money's on Ed. He works for*
*Bear Stearns. On the other hand . . .*

———————

The executive world is a festival of opportunity for those who
love to eat.

Ceremonies surrounding food are, in fact, one of the only
ostensibly business-related events in which too much actual
work is frowned upon. The Four Seasons restaurant, home of

moguls, potentates, heads of state, and assorted war criminals for several generations now, will not even allow the business luncher in the vaunted Grill Room to put pad and paper on the table. Briefcases are not only frowned upon, they are checked downstairs. One is expected to eat, and enjoy the food, and perhaps to chat about appropriate matters of state in a way that does not disturb the digestion. There is a reason why, in the face of all competition, that establishment remains at the top of the food chain, literally.

Members of civilized cultures do not work while they eat. As far as we have now declined in many ways from the more advanced standards of previous generations, there is still a trace memory of this ancient imperative. The implications for us are very positive. It means that the executive who carves out well-defined dayparts for the purpose of business eating, and selects appropriate companions, may create a multiplicity of times during the working day in which the work/nonwork distribution is quite satisfactory for our purposes.

For the person who has yet to establish the entitled zone for herself, each meal represents a certain challenge. Take breakfast, for instance. Those on the front edge of their working retirement may still have a boss who expects them to be in the pocket when the 9 AM whistle blows. Reactions to the player sashaying in at 9:17 with egg yolk on her chin may range from, "Where have YOU been?" to "I was unaware that we were taking a half day today," to the most embarrassing, "You have egg yolk on your chin," delivered with an accusatory scowl.

Executrick no. 1 in this regard is to alter the space/time continuum in which "work" is expected to be done on location. This entails a two-step process where first the concept of "on time" is stretched to accommodate time spent eating and a secondary tier of action in which the authority figure is kept up to date on one's whereabouts until so sick of it that he or she can take it no longer and says, "Whatever." At that point, one is free to judiciously stretch the allotted time for breakfasting, lunching, dining, and even mid-afternoon snacking until it attains quantum brevity.

### EXECUTRICK:
## Setting Up the Legitimate Meal Zone

1. In the beginning, always be on time for each daypart; have meals around those boundaries;

2. Begin adding unassailable companions;

3. Stretch envelope, or better still, push it;

4. When queried, report on company and content of meal;

5. Stretch envelope farther; ask permission for especially lengthy events justified by excellence of companionship;

6. Continue aggressive reporting to point where boss is really bored with it;

7. Attain status as power eater, whose best work is done over a table.

As one makes one's way through a business career, this capacity to extend the concept of the business meal as a form of work grows exponentially. A junior person may be able to push the boundaries, but there are still boundaries. More proficient and daring individuals, after a protracted effort, can achieve truly splendid results, rendering a huge part of the workday impervious to any labor that does not involve a knife and fork.

Obviously, there are nuances in the way that retired working executives use each meal once this zone of comfort has been established. Let's start from the beginning of the day and look at each potential venue, for they are many and splendid indeed.

## Impunity by Daypart

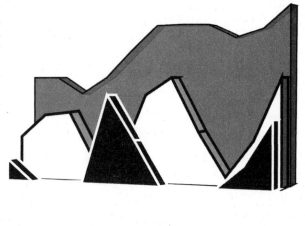

■ Associate ☐ Vice President ▨ CEO

Try to view each of them as an event with a little membrane around it. On the exterior is the rest of the world and its demands. On the inside, with all that tasty mucilage and albumin, is you, having a blast.

Most truly retired people that I have known—the ones condemned to spend an eternity burning in Florida, Arizona, or San Diego—rise with the sun and endure a lonely breakfast in silence and solitude. They are lonely because they have no choice; their selection of breakfast companions is limited to themselves, their spouse, and possibly Ned, Fred, Ed, and Ted down at the club they must attend for fun and golf until they die.

You, on the other hand, have way too many people in your face and are attempting to limit their number and influence on your peace of mind. The experience of a tasty bite at the beginning of the day, undisturbed by anything but the normal aggravation that attends your morning reading, is the consummation of a dream. That is why one of the great, establishing pillars of our program is the simple bagel, muffin (or other pastry), and coffee or tea, taken either behind a closed door in one's office or at a remote location where one cannot be reached for a time. If queried, just say you were at a morning meeting. After a while, you will become known as somebody who has a lot of morning meetings. That's not a bad thing, particularly if you do have some morning meetings now and then. So in order to create the working assumption that you are busy before others are, even though you are not, start scheduling.

## Things to Do When You Breakfast Alone

1. Read the trades;

2. Watch your BlackBerry; issue digital commands;

3. Think;

4. Enjoy your bacon.

Almost as good as the lonely peace of the simple baked good is a splendid repast taken with one of two entities:

1. A friend or pleasant associate;

2. You, eating by yourself because you were "stood up" by somebody who "got their signals crossed."

This last eventuality is not uncommon. People either blow off or sleep through business breakfasts every day, and there are few things as joyful as the realization that the person you're waiting for isn't coming and you'll just have to take the cheese omelet, bacon, four-grain toast, and six cups of coffee all by yourself with a copy of *Variety*. When you return to the office, if anybody wants to know where you were at the opening bell, you can just say, "I was at Michael's waiting for Charlie Roover. Numbnuts never showed."

If Charlie does show, you should make sure that he's not the wrong kind of Roover. I once scheduled a breakfast with a woman who I thought was okay. I knew her when she was a low-level manager at one of our subsidiaries. While she was a little sharp on the draw, I thought she'd be good enough company for an hour or so first thing in the morning. It turned out she had moved on and become the head of Human Resources for a huge Internet service provider who had just taken over a big media company. At that moment, she and her pals at the acquiring party were planning the liquefaction of a horde of poor slobs who they had just taken over. For an hour and a half she regaled me with all the things they were going to do to the idiots and morons and bozos and numbskulls who used to run one of the greatest conglomerates since Rome. Everybody had to go. And the delight she took in her triumphant viciousness first thing in the morning! I had heartburn for three hours afterward.

The other institutional breakfast that is worthwhile is the Bagel with the Boss. By "bagel," by the way, I mean a variety of things and by no means wish to appear regionally or culturally insensitive. Comestibles that may be included under the rubric include:

> The bagel itself, a breadlike object with a hole in the center. The dough of a true bagel is boiled before it is baked. Many "bagels" served in the United States are shaped like bagels but are not true bagels. They may be eaten with cream cheese, although in this particular case

one that is toasted with butter is easier to handle, since you're probably sitting across the desk from your boss and don't want cream cheese squishing all over your tie;

▶ Any sort of muffin. Muffins are a very congenial breakfast substance and convey conviviality if the other person is having a muffin, too; may even be a decent conversation opener when one is needed, as in, "Do you prefer to begin with the tops or the bottoms?"

▶ Toast and English muffins. The English muffin, even if bears the name of muffin, is actually a form of bread, since it must be toasted and not eaten straight out of the bag, rendering it into the toast category ipso facto;

▶ Anything the boss is eating, including even such things as the croissant-wich or Egg McMuffin, which is not a muffin, either, by the way;

▶ Coffee and gum.

The drill is pretty easy. It's best when you are just sort of around when coffee is being slurped and you insouciantly "drop by" with your cup and brown paper bag. If your office is right down the hall from Bob, you may establish a certain regularity in the execution of this trick. You want to be careful, however, that it doesn't take place too often, because that will transform it from a work-eradicating measure into work itself. Anything

## Bagel with the Boss: Topics

1. Golf;

2. Football;

3. What a loser Lazenby is, and what could possibly be done about it;

4. How well young McTavish is doing;

5. The stock price;

6. How advertising is pacing;

7. What a bunch of schmucks the guys over at Omnivore are;

8. Cheese;

9. Horses;

10. The lamb chops at Giovanni's.

done on a schedule as part of your expected duties may be defined as work. So don't get into a rut.

But if managed correctly, the Bagel with the Boss is without question a huge tool, if I may use such indelicate phraseology. It sets up an atmosphere of intimacy first thing in the morning that just might last all day. Not for you is the midday suck-up that a lot of mid-level aspirants feel they need to pull with the big dog. Who needs the five o'clock "accidental" interface with

Bob in the thirty-eighth-floor men's room? Not you. You've had the best possible quality time with the boss, just a few moments before you both suited up for real and put on your faces. That fifteen or twenty minutes buys you an entire day of retirement, possibly even two in slow-moving, industrial organizations.

Breakfast is only one entry point into the Teletubby land of bright colors and easy play. It is a small and perfect preamble, a jewel in the crown of your retirement. Lunch, however, if handled correctly, is an enormous howitzer shell that can take out the entire midsection of your working day. This is not quite as true in the red states of our nation, where sometimes the selection of establishments is rather limited and transit time can be counted in the minutes, with free parking. But in urban locations, particularly Los Angeles, the process of planning for lunch, leaving for lunch, driving to lunch, being seen at lunch, lunching, getting your car, making it back over the hill from lunch, going from your car to your office, and finally returning to your office to begin planning for dinner and tomorrow's meals can destroy the workbed between late morning and mid-afternoon. Other towns, like Chicago, New York, Washington, San Francisco, and, in the winter, Minneapolis, Rochester, and Toronto, not to mention horrible traffic metropolises like London, Paris, Berlin, and of course Rome, all offer, within the confines of their particular cultures, tremendous opportunities in this area. Those thinking of utilizing their expense accounts and network of friends and associates to explore this strategy might consider relocation from areas like Pittsburgh, where there are two restaurants people eat at and about six people to eat with. On the other hand, they do drink at lunch, prodigious tumblers of brain Drano, year after year. So there's that.

After many years investigating this subject, I believe the data points to the following conclusions:

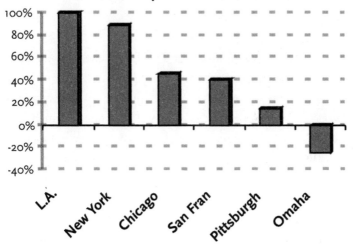

**Potential for Expansion of Lunch Time**

Once the yawning gap of fruitless time is set up and groomed, the inveterate lunching retiree must occupy and fill it in precisely the right fashion. Junior lunchers have a relatively simple agenda, that is, to find a good spot where they will be welcome and a range of companions that are fun enough to be with and make sense on an expense report. Advanced practitioners of the lunching arts have a somewhat more ambitious program to pursue.

First, there comes the job of adopting a few establishments at which one may expect to be treated like a combination of Bill Clinton, Tony Bennett, Donald Trump, and Paris Hilton. This place, and there is at least one in every city where self-important people reside, can be relied upon to provide several things:

▶ Inflated status for people who frequent it;

▶ A sense of community for regulars;

▶ A table thoroughly suitable for the building of one's professional reputation both inside and outside of one's corporate setting;

▶ No surprises and no embarrassing letdowns on busy days;

▶ A certain amount of people-watching recreational value;

▶ Okay food with quick service, particularly at the end of the lunch process when one is yearning for a quick exit.

The acquisition of a proper table—that is, one suitable to your status and perhaps a little better, is an important consideration. It's a form of loyalty that a restaurant gives to people who have shown loyalty to them. This is sometimes not well

## Acquiring a Career-Building Table

*1.* Go to the place every week, perhaps several times a week, and tip well;

*2.* Make reservations every time, never just show up and expect to be squeezed in;

*3.* Make the reservation for a slightly odd hour, perhaps a bit earlier than you might like, at a time when few people are lining up for the lunch yet;

*4.* Now and then, indicate that the person you will be with is "important to you";

*5.* Introduce your companion to the maître d', know all the staff's names;

*6.* If the place can't give you a good table that day, don't fuss, but don't go.

understood. In such places, how famous you might be or how rich you are is less important than how many times you bought the $85 plate of linguini last year and whether you gave the maître d' a Christmas kiss.

Of course, if George Herbert Walker Bush or Ivanka Trump show up, they're likely to get a better table than you, but a good business restaurant will never skunk its regulars, not even if Mick Jagger unexpectedly materializes. The uninitiated sometimes believe that pure rocket power determines the cosmology

## Appetizers: Yes or No?

**1. Do you like your companion? And if so, how much?**

**2. Is there a point, as much as you may like this person across the table, at which you will become sick of them?**

**3. Do you plan to order cookies and coffee for dessert, thus making this a three-act event?**

**4. Is there actual business to conduct here, creating the need for ramping up more length?**

**5. Are there any appetizers you actually like?**

of a hot restaurant. To some extent this is true, especially in places that exist to serve those types. And it makes some sense, if you don't want to be velvet-roped, ever, to avoid such places. That's all right. They'll be gone soon. The true, long-standing institutions know that they will thrive over time only if they treat the people who rely on them for status and career glow with dependable, seemly kissing up. That's the kind of place you want to find. Once you have, grapple it to your soul with hoops of steel. It will become an important part of your pleasant, working retirement.

You may notice at this point that we've been talking about the grand meals of the corporate aristocracy for a while and haven't mentioned a single thing about food. That's because to a large extent business eating, while it perforce involves food, is not about food at all. I eat in a place in New York City a lot that confers a ridiculous amount of buzz and status on me person-ally because I get a good table there. Most of the people who eat there have the same thing every single day: the Cobb salad. It's an okay salad, but they don't eat it because it's okay. They eat it because it's the only thing on the menu they sort of like. I try to vary my choices a little bit and haven't eaten the Cobb salad for a couple of years. Lately, I've tried to stick with the free range chicken, not because I believe in kindness to chickens (although I am not against it) but because it comes with a mountain of French fries. I only eat a couple. But I like them. So are we all going to this place for the food? Not at all, although the food is fine as far as that goes. We're there because it's our lunchroom, that's all, and if you don't protect your table some other kind just might swoop down and get it.

I don't kid myself. I play by the rules. I make my reservation and have a certain range of table that is acceptable to me. And I don't cut too much attitude. Punishment is harsh for those who fail to follow these rather easy guidelines.

Two stories come to mind.

Story No. 1: A couple of years ago, the maître d' at my place seated me at a table behind a certain mirrored post that dissects the room. In front of the mirrored post are hitters. Behind the mirrored post are regular people, faded executives, out-of-work moguls, and guys who look sort of familiar from cable reality shows. I ate lunch just like always, and then, as I was leaving, I took Steve aside and, very calmly and gently, said to him, "Steve,

## Canceling a Lunch Date
## without Prejudice

1. First cancellation: If you've left a few hours to spare, have your assistant do it; it's business, it's not personal;

2. Second cancellation: If it's *really* close in, however, you do it. Be sincere. Say your boss has pulled your chain;

3. Third cancellation: There is no such thing if you want to maintain the relationship. If you don't, there's no better way to kill one.

I know you have a really tough job juggling everybody's egos and all, and I also know that you are superbly attuned to who is who and all that. So I'll just say this. It may be that the day will come when my stock falls low enough that I just can't realistically expect to sit in front of the mirrored post anymore. When that time comes, just tell me and I just won't eat here. It'll break my heart, but I'll get it. Until then, however, please put me in front of the mirrored post when I come here. If you can't for some logistical reason, just tell me. I won't be mad. I'll just go someplace else that day. But my status is so tied at this point to my positioning here that I really can't sustain people seeing me where I was today. Everybody will think I'm totally over. And then I will be. Okay?"

Steve totally understood where I was coming from and so far I've never been behind that mirrored post again. That was three years ago. One time they even put in a card table in a really weird place to accommodate me. I appreciated it. I'm humble in my pride. And I understand what that particular restaurant is all about, and how integral to my developing retirement.

Story No. 2: My friend Botnick was accustomed to sitting at a certain table every time he went to this very same place, well in front of the mirrored post. One day he shows up around 12:15, no reservation. "I'm sorry, Mort," says Steve, who is really a very nice guy and understands how hard Botnick may take this blow to his *amour propre.* "You didn't make a reservation and your table has been assigned to somebody else." Another person might have said, "That's okay, Steve, I'll just take whatever you got. I realize I should have called ahead." But not Botnick. Too large a

---

**EXECUTRICK:**

### *Things You May Refuse to Eat, Even in Asia or France*

1. **Raw liver;**

2. **Raw pigeon egg;**

3. **Raw lobster;**

4. **Raw beef;**

5. **Raw squid;**

6. **Monkey brains;**

7. **Dog.**

part of Botnick's self-image had been invested in his status as permanent resident of Table 14, to the extent, I believe, that like an infant he believed the table ceased to exist when he was not at it. So naturally, he went totally ballistic, declared public war on this institution, which is treasured by all the shallow associates, friends, and colleagues who associate with him both socially and professionally, declaring loudly that he will never go there again! He refused bouquets of flowers that, most disgustingly, were sent to him by the establishment by way of apology, and relocated to a new place stuffed with the same level of pretension but none of the charm or sense of community. I will tell you that, as far as I can tell, his importance within that group of people is now diminished exponentially.

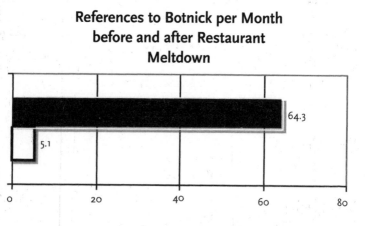

**References to Botnick per Month before and after Restaurant Meltdown**

64.3

5.1

0    20    40    60    80

☐ After Meltdown    ■ Before Meltdown

A word to the wise, then. None of us are bigger than the social milieu that lends us our standing. This is especially true of those whose job description includes vast helpings of tiramisu.

There only remains my responsibility to say a few words about the business dinner. Unless it's a mandatory event of some kind organized by your boss, you're on your own time, you can eat what you want, where you want, when you want to. If the business reason is tenuous, don't go overboard on the cost. If you're taking the president of Wal-Mart out, on the other hand, try the veal. It's the best in the city.

# 5

## The Art and Science of Alcohol

*One man's ceiling
is another man's floor.*
PAUL SIMON

*Christ, was I drunk last night.*
MARK CROWLEY
THE BOYS IN THE BAND

*Oh for God's sake. Cosgrove is going to order Sambuca now. What the hell does he see in the stuff? First we had martinis. Then came wine and then more wine and then some more wine and now everybody's yelling about a nightcap? The room is spinning! And now this? It's all goopy and syrupy and way too sweet! Gotta drink it, though. Guys in Sales will think I'm a weenie if I don't. I remember last year in New Orleans, Moran standing in the middle of Bourbon Street screaming at me, "You're a pussy!" at the top of his lungs because I wanted to go home at 3 AM. That's late! We'd been drinking since cocktails at 6! Jesus, these guys just don't know when to say when. Crazy bastards! I love them! Pass that bottle, fools! I'll show you who's a pussy!*

---

In this area, as in so many others, the virtual retirement supersedes and transcends the real thing that is forced upon the unsuspecting and resistant elderly late in life, when they cannot defend themselves from this onslaught of mandatory inactivity. If old people drink like Cossacks, they end up dead with their faces in the rice pudding. If strong, healthy players in the prime of a business career do it, they become legends.

Those who do not make the most of the rolling, spouting river of first-class liquor that inhabits executive life are missing one of the most happy and productive areas of their ersatz retirement. Those who do not employ the most sophisticated executricks to help them manage this great asset are, however, likely to spiral into destruction. The great tragedy of alcoholism is that it forces one to stop drinking. This, in turn, renders much professional life intolerable.

Any visit to a well-stocked bar, tavern, or alcoholic's rumpus room will evince the vast and stunning array that humanity has assembled for the purpose of self-inebriation. Some are appropriate to a business venue. Sadly, others are not. Before we go much further, let's take a look at some of the choices available to you and how they stack up in the workplace environment for our purposes.

## Your Drink: Yes or No

| BEVERAGE | YES/NO | COMMENT |
| --- | --- | --- |
| Scotch | Yes | Manly for either gender |
| Bourbon | Yes | Watch your gut, Gomer |
| Rye | Yes | Very '60s |
| Vodka | Yes | The choice of alcoholics everywhere |
| Gin | No | Businessperson's LSD |
| Martini | Yes | *Sophistiqué!* |
| Crème de menthe | No | What are ya, a sissy? |

| BEVERAGE | YES/NO | COMMENT |
|---|---|---|
| Brandy | Yes | End of evening only |
| Beer | Yes | On the rocks after 2 AM |
| Ale | No | Only for Tudors |
| Wine | Yes | When your nose turns red, it's time to stop |
| Sangria | Problematic | Only in Spain or if others are drinking it |
| Anisette | No | Unless you're Uncle Junior |
| Sambuca Romano | Yes | Way, way after dinner, and only a little, unless you want to wake up with a dead badger in your mouth |
| Curaçao/Kahlúa, etc. | No | Are you on your prom? |
| Ouzo | No | Beware of Greeks bearing it |
| Grappa | Yes | To show you're a big tough business operator |

Some notes here:

▶ Never get drunk on beer. It's jejune. You may drink it, of course, but don't drink enough to get burping, braying drunk. This is not a frat house party. This is business.

▶ All rules are moot if the boss is drinking it. I had a CEO one time who liked mead, for chrissake. So I drank mead. Unless you're a Viking of some kind, it's pretty horrible.

▶ Ouzo is impossible to drink without getting really silly. It almost always makes people tear off their ties and wear them around their heads. Regrettable things follow.

▶ Grappa, on the other hand, is a better choice, because no one can really down too much of it. Grappa is a clever plot by southern Europeans to take used or substandard battery acid and repackage it as a beverage. It goes immediately to the corpus callosum of your brain, the part that keeps your rational side in communication with your nutty, expressive side, and cuts all discourse. You have a grappa and then go home.

▶ I have already indicated my distaste for Sambuca Romano. It is, however, a ceremonial drink for many. Refusal of a glass, when it is offered, is the equivalent of failing to belch after a tasty plate of roast schnauzer in Beijing.

▶ Martinis are a wonderful drink for business. People think you're all kinds of cute and smart if you drink them. You look 15 percent more intelligent just holding one. You look just as sharp with your second. After your third, you will almost certainly be a sloshy moron trying to hump the nearest credenza. Moderation in all hard liquor is a good idea, but there is a tipping point with martinis that must be respected.

▶ Liqueurs are for sissies.

There is much more to consider about each of the potables that God has graciously given to us. This is not a book, however, about the wonder and mystery of alcohol per se but about how you can incorporate the stuff into your working life, and to do so without falling over either metaphorically or physically.

So let's look at the business day and the opportunities and pitfalls it offers.

I'm sorry to say that as the world changes we are forced to change with it. Movies from the 1930s to the 1960s feature

---

### EXECUTRICK:
## *Excuses for Drinking at Breakfast*

*1.* You're with another alcoholic;

*2.* Nothing to do that day until noon at least;

*3.* Having a huge breakfast that will cancel effects;

*4.* Celebrating something with the boss;

*5.* You're on your last legs and just don't give a crap anymore.

---

thoroughly capable and civilized people smoking like fiends and drinking at breakfast in order to straighten themselves out after big benders the night before, drinking at mid-morning, drinking during meetings, drinking big, sweaty martinis at lunch, drinking, drinking, drinking, and the only people who were looked at funny were those who couldn't "hold their liquor," a notoriously imprecise phrase that could mean anything from hitting on the chairman's wife at a banquet to hurling at the Christmas party. Short of that, you were pretty much okay. If you need any proof of this, rent one of the old movies, like *The Thin Man* starring William Powell. He was urbane. He was witty. He put away, by my count, between nine and twelve martinis a day. Or, if you're more the macho type, consider the western. How many shots per reel does John Wayne or Clint Eastwood slam back in one of those horse operas? But we? We are referred to the corporate Employee Assistance Program if we have a screwdriver with breakfast or a glass of wine at lunch. Ah, the forest of Pellegrino bottles that litter the tables of the rich and mighty! What a load.

The truth is, this nation grew faster and produced more every day when it was halfway potted all the time. A few years ago, when advertising was growing 8–10 percent per year, for a period of decades, the Sales Department of my corporation was staffed by a bunch of total gonzo maniacs. The most restrained among them were the ones who simply drank and did not snort cocaine. When a big client came to town from, say, Detroit, the drill went like this:

▶ Come in around 10 AM and do the whole "Christ, was I drunk last night" thing;

▶ Meet the client for lunch. Drinking begins;

▶ Lunch is over. Go to another bar and drink more until dinnertime;

▶ Dinnertime arrives. Steaks are eaten. Flagons of wine are consumed along with after-dinner beverages;

▶ Everybody goes to another nightclub for a while to chill out and drink more;

▶ Strip joint, more booze;

▶ After-hours place. Substances that help you stay awake. Drink all night;

▶ At around 8 AM, a new shift of Sales guys comes into the office just as the old, wasted crew is about to drop. The fresh team then leaves the office to join the client for breakfast, letting the nearly dead crew go home but never leaving the client unattended;

▶ This goes on, with a fresh shift relieving those about to drop, as long as the client is in town.

If you're wondering how "business" got done, I will say that one guy, usually a vice president of some importance, remained in the office all the previous day and in the morning so that the phones would be answered and non-Sales executives could be served if need be. But the real answer is that the true business was not being done in the office. It was being done in the restaurants, bars, and dance emporia.

Homey don't play that anymore. I don't know of a single company that plays host to those kinds of idiotic shenanigans. And our growth rates are about 10 percent of what they were when the whole world was walking around smoked up and blasted.

Be that as it may, we have to live in this world and not in the past, so the sad fact is that you can't really drink at breakfast except for some very specific reasons noted above. You'll just have to eat and get as jazzed as you can on caffeine. There are worse things.

Harder, however, is the current Calvinist attitude about drinks at lunch. For grown people, particularly adults in their forties and fifties, this stricture seems trendy, foolish, and, actually, counterintuitive to a productive business environment. Should all business be done by sober people who have all their inhibitions intact? I think not. Throughout world history, decisions great and small were made not by the people who went around drinking water with every meal. In fact, in medieval and Renaissance England, when the greatest empire since Rome (where they subsisted on lots and lots of wine) was being built, the water was so lousy that people drank a gross, sludgy form of low-alcohol ale from morning until night. Perhaps continuing in that great British tradition, Winston Churchill drank a gallon or so of brandy every day while conducting the most serious business of the twentieth century. You know who I'm sure doesn't drink at lunch? Vladimir Putin. I bet he's very sober.

Anyhow, what's the point of whining about the gross sobriety that has overtaken us? The reality is that it takes a courageous and highly effective executive to order a glass of wine with his or her lunch at this point in history. And, in my view, hard liquor is absolutely OUT for all but the most flamboyant moguls or high-priced defense attorneys, the kinds of guys who make their own rules.

Our job, on the other hand, is quite different than theirs. Ours is not to make our own code of conduct, but rather to create the solid impression that we are living within the confines of existing norms while doing basically whatever we please. We are after freedom, not license. So no liquor license for you, Sport.

That does not mean, however, that the envelope within which we live is sealed. I will hereby suggest the implementation of a new standard. From this time forth, I believe we should all begin to order a glass of wine with lunch. If people won't have a glass of wine with you—don't eat lunch with them again. By 2012, it is possible, if we work very hard and stick by our strategy in this regard, that we may be at a point where a bottle of wine between friends will be back in vogue.

There is, thank goodness, a tradition still extant of people in business getting together for drinking lunches on special occasions—birthdays, retirements (genuine), New Year's, July

## Drinking at Lunch

*1.* No excuse needed unless you are with a very dry senior officer;

*2.* No spirits unless your companion is having one;

*3.* Wine is fine; good wine even better;

*4.* Limit of one unless . . .

> *a.* You're a very heavy hitter;
>
> *b.* Your companion joins you;
>
> *c.* You're on your last legs and you just don't give a crap.

Fourth, the closing of big deals, summer Fridays, Memorial and Labor Day getaway days, and of course the two to three weeks around December/January holiday time, to name just a few. These events merge with the sacrosanct business dinner, and the elastic, plastic ritual of cocktails, to present certain issues to the happily working retiree. For while these occasions continue on as strong as ever, people nowadays sneer at anybody who actually appears drunk in public. There is a snobby, tragically erroneous belief that simply because a person gets a bit frosted in a social situation now and then, they are, ipso facto, a rummy, a tosspot, and a tippler, and therefore not to be trusted as an executive.

You must therefore watch the way you express your *joie de vivre* while in your cups. In a business context, an unacceptable level of inebriation is made up of certain discrete elements that come together to form the entire pie of disgrace:

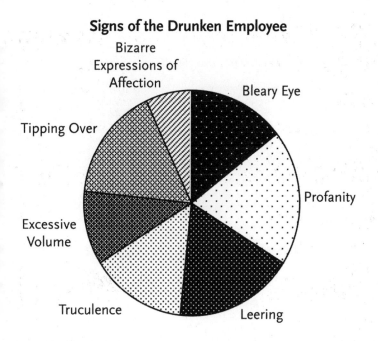

**Signs of the Drunken Employee**

I once attended a major industry cocktail party at one of my favorite restaurants. It might even have been the one I talked about in the last chapter. I made several mistakes before the party.

## EXECUTRICK:

# How to Drink a Lot without Appearing Unacceptably Drunk

1. Drink the same thing all night;

2. Eat three hors d'oeuvres for every drink;

3. Have one club soda for every three drinks;

4. Do NOT drink more than five tumblers of anything;

5. Find a boring group of people and stand by them for a while;

6. If you feel that you love someone, do not tell them;

7. If you feel like hitting someone, do not hit them;

8. If you feel like hurling, leave;

9. If you are asked to leave, leave;

10. Remember: You don't need a weatherman to know which way the wind blows.

1. I met a friend for drinks beforehand and, during the conversation, which went on for at least an hour, had not one but two martinis. These were not your 1950s-style martinis of perhaps four or five ounces with a little green olive impaled on a dime-store toothpick. These were the kind they serve at 21, which provides basically enough liquid in which to take a sponge bath.

## Drinking with Lightweights

*1.* Allow the heaviest lightweight to order. He will probably go for white wine;

*2.* Drink the white wine;

*3.* When all the lightweights are slightly inebriated, order what you want;

*4.* Don't get overserved.

2. For some reason when I finally reached the party I was tired of martinis and switched over to scotch. This is not advisable, I know that, and all I can say in my defense is that I'd had two martinis already and nothing to eat and somehow it seemed like a credible decision. So I had a couple of stiff brown drinks in a matter of minutes.

3. At that point it's all kind of a blur to me. I do remember telling a reporter from the *New York Times* to go fuck himself, in what I believed to be a good-natured way. I also made a lunch date for the next day with a corporate behemoth I've known for about twenty years. He's a friend, but also a boss of mine. When I failed to show up for our lunch the next day (it had for some reason totally slipped my mind), he called and asked me if I had

considered seeing a mental health care professional. I told him I already did.

4. My last memory of the party is of the restaurant owner, who is a good guy but also, you know, the owner of the establishment on which I rely for fully 52 percent of my credibility as an industry executive, putting a friendly arm around my shoulders and walking me out of the place.

I had to attend no fewer than six separate public events in the next few months in total sobriety to undo the impression that I had some kind of a drinking problem.

It just goes to show that the specter of self-immolation is never all that far away. And it could ruin everything if you allow it to achieve corporeal reality.

---

**EXECUTRICK:**

## Drinking with Heavyweights

1. Be a middleweight;

2. Watch the bozos;

3. Have a nice bite to eat. Drink what you want;

4. Don't mind if they call you a pussy. They are pussies who need to be shitfaced in order to operate;

5. Core concept: They can drink more than you can. Don't try to keep up.

---

Let moderation in excess be your byword!

This is most easily effected by a reliance on wine, since if you've been drinking with an eye for the long ball since your teens like most of us, you can handle your wine pretty well in both a personal and, more important, a business context. I have known extremely powerful people who consume as much wine as a Tuscan village while pulling off billion-dollar transactions. That's because while hard liquor fries the brain, wine—especially the kind of excellent wine to which even your average executive has access—only lightly poaches the cerebellum. And while all of us need to get fried now and then, particularly those who eat stress with their corn flakes, the tender braising that wine offers is a much better life choice over time.

Good Lord, there are millions of books on wine, and a multiplicity of pompous, red-nosed colleagues who can out-wine you at this point. That doesn't mean you can't, with a good Platinum Card and a lenient controller, explore the valley of the grape and come away with purple teeth and a merry heart. And you don't have to be a snooty sommelier to get the job done.

In fact, I'd like to ask all of you wine dudes to leave the room now. I'm talking to all my fellow idiots out there.

Restaurants generally bump up the price of a bottle of wine by 300 percent. That means a bottle of wine you order at a decent dinner establishment for $100 would set you back between $25 and $35 at a local store. I don't know about you, but a wine that costs me anything more than $20 at a store is a good wine. If my palate was a person, it would have an IQ of 110. And I have done nothing to cultivate or enrich it all that much. I consider its average status to be one of the greatest assets I possess at any business function. Whatever they're pouring, for the most part, I can drink.

While it is all right to appear uninitiated, however, it is not permissible to play the drooling fool on any subject, even wine. That is why, as a public service, I will now give you some acceptable comments you can use when presented with an offensive wine-related situation.

First, I'm going to assume that you let Rudolph and the rest of his red-nosed crew do the ordering. You're not a total numbskull, are you? Let the wine guys have their fun! This leaves you with nothing more than the responsibility to not disgrace yourself with some stupid remark that could designate you as an individual not worthy to drink the nectar that is being ordered.

What you want, more than anything, is to find yourself in the midst of a bunch of wine weenies trying to outshine each other. That happened to me at Emeril's in New Orleans a few years back, where two guys, both worth more than the GNP of Bosnia, each was trying to outorder the other. By the time we were done, more than $20,000 worth of wine had gone down our throats, on their inevitable way into the sea. I was honored to be there. And truthfully, I was at a loss for what to say in the awesome shadow of all that fine wine. In retrospect, here is what I now feel would have been appropriate.

| SITUATION | APPROPRIATE COMMENT |
|---|---|
| Wine is presented. | "What is this, guys? Tell me a little about it." |
| Wine is poured. | "Wow. That smells good." |
| Wine guys swirling, smacking. | Taste wine. Remain mute. |
| Wine guys comment. | Appear interested. |
| Wine guys drink. | Drink. |
| Bottle is empty. | "Boy. That went fast! Is there more?" |

If this seems like a pageant of stupidity on the subject, don't worry. Remember that the hallmark of a great businessperson is the ability to know what he or she doesn't know. Also, like nuclear physicists or brain surgeons, wine guys love to talk about their passionate enthusiasm. So you can never go wrong just enjoying the grape and asking them to tell you about it. After a while, God help us all, you will find yourself growing interested, and be able to offer remarks about the plangency of its nose, or the robustness of its shoulders, its chocolate undertones or woody audacity, nonsense like that.

You may try to resist, but the dirty, ugly truth is that talk about booze is very interesting to anybody who likes to drink it, and if that's your boss, your client or your colleagues, conversation on the subject may postpone business talk perpetually. Better still, eventually, you will give in and start to enjoy wine for the right reasons, i.e., it tastes good, softens the world, and gets you loaded. You also rarely get into really bad trouble on wine, unless you think falling asleep at the table is a cardinal career sin.

I do hope, for your sake and that of your expense account, that no matter how astute or impassioned you get on the subject, you never lose your ability to enjoy a nice, average wine. We're not talking Boone's Farm. But a $15 bottle of Zin from Sonoma should always be able to float your boat. When it doesn't, you may be on your way to being the kind of person you used to despise. I hope you have the plastic to support it.

I realize that I've spent the best part of this discussion on warnings, admonitions, and other disagreeable stuff like that. That's because the ability, once again, to exert control over the source of your various enjoyments is what separates the gainfully retired from the folks who used to sit in front of the mirrored post, if you remember back that far in this exercise.

If you don't, you've been drinking too much, pal. Cut back.

# 6

## Travel on Plastic

*Let us eat and drink,*
*for tomorrow we die.*
ISAIAH 22:13

*May the road rise up to meet you as you go.*
IRISH TOAST

*It's so quiet in here. The bed is huge. The curtains are thick and plush and encase me like a big, friendly bosom. I like this bathrobe, too. Very cozy. I don't have anything to do until tomorrow, and even then it's mostly sitting around. I love hotels. This is a particularly superb one, too. They upgraded me to a suite, because I'm such a good customer. I think I'll run the hot tub and go in there for a while. But first, maybe a few of these Godivas from the minibar and some of those luscious plums from the complimentary basket the manager arranged for me. Got to remember to call down for a wake-up call tomorrow morning. The Town Car will be here to get me at eight. I want to have time for breakfast before that. I could go to the Club here on the eighteenth floor. It's very plush, with acres of tasty tidbits both hot and cold and refreshing drinks of all kinds. But I think I'll have cottage cheese pancakes and applewood sausage in the room here. Also I should probably pack and let Jerry keep my bag in the trunk of the limo. By this time tomorrow, I'll be in the air, eating the warm nuts and having two or three Glenlivets. I wonder what the weather is like back home right now. On the other hand, who cares?*

—————

One of the downsides of real retirement, and why it is generally wasted on the generally penurious elderly, is the expense of travel for all but the very, very rich. Even those, when they get on in years, generally are more concerned with their proximity to a working bathroom than they are with seeing Berbers riding like the wind across the desert or tasting the wild nightlife of Marseilles or Pittsburgh. Don't scoff. Pittsburgh's a hot town if you find the right places. There are, I believe, three, unless one of them has closed.

Be that as it may, the executive in command of unchallenged plastic may quite literally suck the sweet oyster of international culture down in great drafts. London! Paris! Dubuque! It depends on your business. But you don't have to be in the glittering capitals of the globe to glom on to a bodacious retirement vibe.

The first challenge for he or she who wishes to start sucking that oyster is the barrier that exists, at least in the early part of an effective career, between those who have the right to travel at will and those who do not. The problem is that only those who have proven themselves highly effective are presumed fit to spread their excellence elsewhere. At the same time, those who have proven themselves highly effective are valued by bosses back at the office, who use them to get out of work. So when you leave the office to travel, you are often making it necessary for your senior officer to work, thus interrupting his or her on-the-job retirement.

The implications of this are clear. For some good long time, and possibly forever unless you rise to a level of truly ultrasenior management, you will need to prove your value to the boss while you are not in the pocket. This means creating sometimes

## Amount of Work the Boss Has to Do
## When You Are Out of the Office

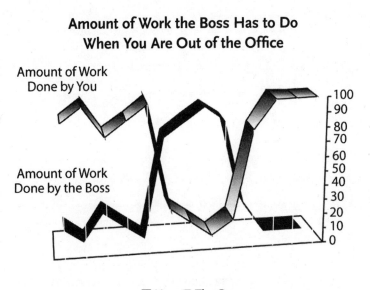

Amount of Work
Done by You

Amount of Work
Done by the Boss

100
90
80
70
60
50
40
30
20
10
0

▨ You  ■ The Boss

false problems to which you can be the solution only if you go to the source of the conflagration. You may also investigate potential trips your superior may be forced to make in the near future, and go there. This is perhaps the quickest way to his or her heart and will establish your right to use plastic on the road to the benefit of the ones in the corner offices. It may, however, land you in some very cold places in the winter.

That said, you've got to start someplace. The executive on his way to a happy working retirement must come and go as he or she pleases. This does not mean that the need to keep Authority informed of your whereabouts altogether disappears,

## Establishing Your Value When You Are Not in the Pocket

*1.* Find a crisis. There is generally one going on somewhere;

*2.* If a crisis is not on hand, find a personnel situation that needs your adjudication in a far-flung location—a firing, a key hiring, etc.;

*3.* Establish the gravity of the situation with your boss;

*4.* Having created the impression of a problem that needs to be solved, you may go and solve it yourself, since no one else will do;

*5.* Make sure to stay in touch, at least in the early years. In fact, pepper your boss with so much incoming he starts avoiding your communications for a while;

*6.* Make sure to have a lot of fun with the locals, on your nickel. Word will get around that you're okay and other field offices will start asking you when you're planning on a visit;

*7.* You may then begin to schedule trips at the request of the field. There is no greater imperative for a corporate operation;

*8.* If you are in the field, reverse direction and begin to work toward eliciting requests from corporate;

*9.* Post-trip, make sure the boss knows all about it.

ever, except for those who either own the company or have otherwise climbed to the stratosphere of institutionalized irresponsibility.

Also, be aware that your modus operandi on the road will change over time. When I began traveling for business, I stayed in nicer Marriotts and even the occasional Best Western. I went to places like Irving, Texas, and the Quad Cities in Iowa. I made sure to eat in modest beaneries and dine with only the most boring and defensible companions. I did not watch in-room movies—a notorious flag for controllers trying to justify their existence. I didn't snack from the minibars. But it was all money in the bank when it came to establishing the creds, the chops, and the techniques I today use to squeeze every last legitimate drop of Grand Marnier from the bonbon of corporate life away from home.

Once you have established the idea of yourself as a provider of solutions to remote problems, you still have a lot of spadework to do before your garden flowers in places you might like to visit. You have to get the knack of acquiring approvals for the trips themselves, timing the requests correctly, and not getting the reputation for being a jerk-off who's never around when you need him.

Keep in the front of your mind that business travel, while it includes the kind of boondoggles we will look at shortly, is not in itself to be considered inherently frivolous or discretionary, as would be, say, an industry convention at which one has no

## *Approvals and Timing*

*1.* **Formal approach: e-mail request, laying out problem, need for trip, length of stay. Indicate availability for further discussion if needed. If no push-back, go ahead and plan;**

*2.* **Brisk, operational approach: in midst of other verbal business, flip in hamburger of approval. If it is downed without incident, you're on;**

*3.* **If resistance is offered, be prepared to stick to guns until annoyance point is reached. Past that, quit and come back;**

*4.* **At the outset, the right to travel is a campaign. Don't make each battle a war. Live to fight another day;**

*5.* **If you must start with day trips to local operations, or even half-days, do so;**

*6.* **Timing: DO NOT disappear during crunch times. People will hate you. If you don't know when those times are, find out;**

*7.* **DO NOT travel to go to parties until you have reached an executive level of power and fatuity;**

*8.* **When you have a trip planned, stick to it. Have courage. It's worth it.**

formal appointments. Those exist and have merit, with the possible exception of the strippers. What we are attempting to establish here is a *life in motion* that can be supported by the State.

In all you do, as you move forward toward that goal, you must be impeccable, both in the rationale for your travel and in its execution, so that you eventually move to the point where you no longer have to have every trip approved. This status, merged with the electronic technologies discussed earlier, render the very best at the game into mysterious figures who are everywhere and nowhere at once. They cruise the lovely places of the globe, modern-day Sir Francis Drakes, privateers on the queen's plastic looking for profit and adventure. The yo-ho-ho and bottle of rum are included.

Let's say you have mastered the basics and created the notion of yourself as a member of the club of professional nomads. You'll go nuts if you have to go here, go there, never really landing in any one spot for very long. That's no fun. You want to go places where everybody knows your name, particularly the people who run the nice hotels you want to stay in. You also want to avoid the early-state status as everybody's dogsbody, going to all the places where nobody else wants to go.

To do this, you will need to set up Zones of Operation to which you may be expected to repair with some regularity. This does two things: first, it gives you multiple bases and ports of call in which you are respected as a person of standing; second, and perhaps more important, it takes you a big step closer to that unquestioned status of which we dream. "Where's Fred?" someone back at home might say. "Schenectady," another will reply, and then everybody will nod. Of course, Fred is in Schenectady. Fred goes there every now and then. Why? We don't know. Who cares? He has business in Schenectady. Good old Fred. Hardworking Fred. Poor guy is almost never around anymore. What a trouper!

See? Fred has established the unquestioned authority to be in Schenectady whenever he wants to. Although we certainly hope, wherever he is, it's not really Schenectady.

I'll give you an example of what I mean. I'm thinking of a certain corporation I know. The accompanying chart indicates where it has legitimate operations, along with the allures of each location:

| CITY | ATTRACTIONS |
|------|-------------|
| New York | Restaurants, theaters, bars, museums, great hotels, feeling of being at the center of the world |
| Los Angeles | Cool scene; no personal accountability for whereabouts; nobody works after 3:30 PM due to abuse of time zone |
| Chicago | Great steak, city of big shoulders |
| London | Incredible energy, constant drafts of very good beer, hilarious English dudes, rockin' hotels |

| CITY | ATTRACTIONS |
|---|---|
| San Francisco | Great weather most of the time, lovely scenery, '60s work ethic abides; possibility of leaving heart there |
| Washington, D.C. | Virtually none as far as I can tell |
| Miami | Mind-boggling night scene; very nice in the winter |
| Tokyo | Totally awesome, all the time, weird and trippy, so far away that what happens there not only stays there but, to some extent, never actually occurred at all |
| Las Vegas | All of the above, plus genuine possibility of total destruction of self as we know it |
| Phoenix/Scottsdale/Carefree | Golf; big-time spa culture |
| St. Louis | Arch, and . . . ? |

Obviously, the availability of all these remote locations to a bored, deskbound executive or someone wishing to emulate one, is like the scent of bacon to a hungry dog, with the possible exclusion of St. Louis. Each represents a potential Zone of Operation. You cannot, however, simply declare a tantalizing destination a work location. You'll get busted if you do. You need, instead, to meet some very specific criteria that fuse over time to provide the necessary credibility to the place to render it habitable as an out-of-home office:

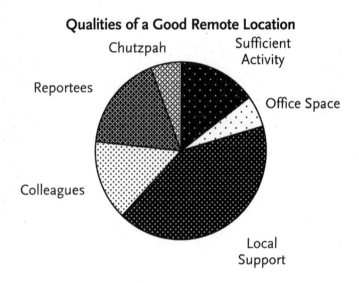

**Qualities of a Good Remote Location**

Chutzpah
Sufficient Activity
Reportees
Office Space
Colleagues
Local Support

Even a cursory glance at this makeup gives you an indication of the time and effort necessary to make someplace in which you are not defined as a resident worker into one where not only are you accepted, you're expected. It may never be possible for you to achieve 100 percent success in any given locale, particularly one as prestigious as London or Los Angeles. But even partial success is worthwhile. To stroll the hallways of an office in Tokyo or San Diego without people looking you up and

## First, Business, or Coach?

*1.* **Never fly coach for any flight over 90 minutes. If they want to send you, they can pay for you to live like a goddamn human being;**

*2.* **If you must fly in steerage, try JetBlue or some other airline where everybody is equal. You'll feel better, and besides, they have TVs;**

*3.* **Don't fly First unless you are officially authorized to do so; if there is any question, don't even ask. Fly Business;**

*4.* **Don't fly First unless it's a flight over 4 hours. The quality difference is minimal and if you abstain, you will get a reputation as a frugal person, even if you're not;**

*5.* **In short, just fly Business. There's no difference except, possibly, that there are more assholes in First and the nuts are slightly hotter.**

down with a narrow expression and saying, "What are you doing here?" is a wonderful feeling, and one that, throughout your career, you should be striving for.

Whether you are moving between your recognized Zones of Operation or simply wading through your company's spheres of influence as an ersatz bona-fide troubleshooter, there are rules of the road that will help you get the most out of your retirement.

Let's begin with your trip to the airport. This is one of the times when just about everybody is entitled to take a Town Car. The question is, what kind of limo are you going to get? There are some limo companies that are inferior to taking a burro. Our goal, lest we forget, is not just to enjoy perks or soak up luxury. It is to achieve the peace of mind and relaxation attendant upon a nice, cushy retirement. If a limousine confers discomfort, bad smells, confusion, and other stressful experiences, you might as well take a nice, quiet bus, right?

Personally, after years of sitting in traffic on the way to Kennedy Airport in New York City, chewing at the inside of my esophagus while the clock ticks ever-closer to my departure time, twitching and sighing in an enclosed space until I want to scream for more than two hours as we creep our way the ten miles to our destination, I now take the E train. Takes me an hour, door to door. Never hangs me up. I just sit there with my little iPod on and it's sixty minutes of silence, 100 percent wi-fi free. No mall-walking nonagenarian in south Florida achieves greater isolation.

I realize that the idea of taking public transport is counterintuitive to our general effort. But there's no rule against creativity and flexibility. And when you get right down to it, don't retired people always take the bus?

In this case, I also believe that the ability to be free of discomfort and to impose an electronic blackout trumps our customary mandate for executive opulence.

Still, status-conscious business wheezebags like us didn't get into this thing to mingle with the hoi polloi. And here, as it so often turns out, it's all about relationships.

## Excuses of Bad Limo Companies

*1.* "He's there. Where are you?"

*2.* "He's at the corner of Smith and Hawkin right around the corner. Five minutes."

*3.* . . . rings . . . (no answer) . . .

*4.* "He's at the corner. You should be able to see him right about now."

*5.* "He's on the Fifty-third Street side. Where are you?"

*6.* "A policeman made him move again."

*7.* "He was there. You must have missed him."

*8.* "We still have to bill you even if you did end up taking a cab."

Do you know the dispatchers of your limo company on a first-name basis? Do you tip them at the jolly time of year? Do you give your limo company a lot of business? Even . . . personal business that of course you do NOT put on your expense account—unless you are a really self-destructive dolt . . .

This is as good a place as any to get this message out of the way: Only shit-for-brains cheat on their expense account. The possibility for *legitimate* abuse is so ample. Who needs that kind of help? Losers, that's who.

Generally, I believe, people who grossly abuse their expense accounts have some other kind of life-crisis going on. A divorce. A gambling problem. Drink. Money. Are you one of those? Bending the ECONOMIC rules, the ones that the . . . financial people . . . care about? Are you crying out to be caught? To be put on real retirement? Because . . . you will be. Out in the cold. Jumped the shark. Sucking the hose.

On the other hand, people do make honest mistakes. Make sure all yours are honest and you should be all right.

Okay, now that we've got that unpleasant subject behind us, let's look at ways we can peel the onion as we go through our day.

**Your limo company is your friend.** No blandishments can be too much. Enough is not enough. You want these guys to be there, on time, with a clean vehicle, a nice driver who either speaks or doesn't, depending on you, and who knows how to go as fast as possible without getting stopped or killed. The guy's driving should not scare you, but he should be, you know, efficient. I don't know about you, but when I'm sitting in the backseat, and I know I could be getting there faster, with less traffic, I feel like jumping across the divider and seizing the steering wheel myself. And yet I can't. It's just not done.

So I maintain a very respectful, even fearful relationship with Donna and Walter and the gang down at Executive Limo. Hi, guys!

**Airport lounging:** All airlines you're likely to spend any time on have a lounge for their business types. I have a special affection for the American Airlines Admiral's Clubs. Come to think

# Bad Limo Drivers I Have Known

*1.* Phil: Long-standing relationship; very unreliable, great raconteur, though. One day failed to show up for a ride to the airport due to a "misunderstanding" consisting solely of the fact that he misunderstood that he needed to be on time. Then he came to my house and threatened to punch me out if I didn't pay for the ride anyway, thus losing a 10-year customer over a $40 dispute.

*2.* George: A very nice person. Took the longest and slowest way toward any destination, but was too proud to be directed. Always knew what he was doing, until he didn't. Eventually, I would yell at him and feel bad afterward. Who needs that kind of emotional investment in the driver?

*3.* Ed: Couldn't stop calling me "Big Guy." I don't like to be called Big Guy. I'm not that big a guy. I still fit into my suits.

*4.* Nachman: Just couldn't stop talking and talking and talking and talking and talking and talking and talking and talking.

*5.* Unknown driver: I hailed him on the street in desperation when another Town Car failed to show up. After about five minutes in traffic, he said, "Excuse me," pulled over, and peed in a bottle. I got out.

of it, now that I've said hi to the limo guys I'd like to take a moment to give a shout-out to all my pals at the Admiral's Club in San Francisco, too! Hi, Dee! It's me! Bing!

I'm actually making a point here, while I also take a second to say what's up to the sleek, handsome group that makes the First Class Admiral's Club at LAX just about the swankiest place to hang out and do e-mail anywhere.

After you settle into a transit groove, you'll start getting to know people all along your route. Many of them are service providers. They will make your life either a dreamy breeze on a flying carpet, or a slog through a pile of ooze. Your choice.

If you're not an Admiral, or a USAir President, or a United Airline Smurf or whatever, see if you can use your plastic to get on board one of these swell digs, even if some are more swell than others. Some are crowded. Others have nothing but pretzels. The one in Paris is too hot all the time. But they still beat sitting on the floor plugged into the wall like R2D2 or ambling about spending money on stupid stuff just to stay awake. And the good ones are islands you can perch on for a bit before you fly away to more substantial aspects of your evolving status.

**Welcome to the hotel, your retirement villa:** They will clean your clothing. They will wake you in the morning. Bring you tasty things to your room. There's a nice TV. You can even turn off the phone. And it's all paid for by the proprietors of your friendly Corporate Home. Who needs a pension? It's a good thing HR took them all away in 2001, huh?

## *Turning a Hotel into a Retirement Villa*

1. Always stay at the same place in every city;

2. Tip high/moderate; be friendly to staff, but not chummy;

3. If after a couple of visits they don't seem to recognize you, go elsewhere;

4. Have an assistant or somebody pretending to be one make all arrangements;

5. Change rooms if you don't like your room; if you feel really pissed off, change it again until you're happy;

6. After the first room service disaster, ass must be kicked. Response to ass-kicking determines future relations;

7. You can always tell the villa that's right for you by how much you like its bar;

8. Spa;

9. Fabulous minibar;

10. Free fruit sometimes.

I don't know that there's a whole lot to add to it. The only problems come to people who don't see their hotels as retirement villas but as rooming houses where they park temporarily, warped dimensions in which they wander aimlessly through the kind of alternate universes string theorists make up. If you doubt what I'm saying, spend a couple of nights in a Japanese hotel the size of a linen closet.

Come with me into one such establishment. That's right. Don't be afraid. You'll live.

> *The temperature is weird. It's hot in places and cold in others. The window doesn't really close right. Where's that wind coming from? It smells funny. It's the odor of last night, but not your last night, somebody else's. Cigar? Booze. Flowers. What are we looking out at? A brick wall. Or a blasted urban terrain, like the surface of the moon, only with parking lots. When you ask to be waked in the morning, they forget. It's like they don't care. They can't change your room if you don't like the Murphy bed, because there are just no extra rooms in the whole 1,200-room hotel. Yeah, right. They're just mean and don't see how being nice is really part of their jobs anyhow. Breakfast was very, very late, too, and they forgot that you don't like cream in your coffee, you specifically asked for milk. Of course, it's no big deal . . . but it's not like home, not at all. In fact, being in places like this makes you homesick. . . .*

Retirement villas, on the other hand! They are staffed by people who care all about everything your teeny-weeny heart desires, because you work so hard, don't you, and you deserve the very, very best. A great hotel is all about making every single person there feel that everything there is being done just for them. For those who love the sand and sea, it's not hard to find such places. Others favor tiny hideaways in large, unfriendly cities. They're out there, too, in every expense-account size. Go find them. Make them your own.

Finally, of course, there is the plastic itself, the physical embodiment of all that you have achieved, the umbilical cord via which all the nutrients from Mother flow.

Respect your plastic. Use it wisely and well. Make other people pay for things now and then, but don't be afraid to test its strength, to work it out so that it gets stronger and more generous year after year. It was not put on the earth, however, to ensure your happiness. It's there to help you do business. So do business, okay?

Don't forget!

# 7

## On Boondoggles

*The rule of my life is to make business
a pleasure, and pleasure my business.*
AARON BURR

*The world, that understandable
and lawful world, was slipping away.*
WILLIAM GOLDING
LORD OF THE FLIES

*Look at Harry over there. He's, what, five-eight, tops, 250 pounds before breakfast. Looks okay in his usual pinstripe and wing tips, but he's not in those now. He's in old Keds, must be from before the Flood. Gray sweatshorts. My, look how white his legs are. And a bright yellow T-shirt that has on it the theme of our boondoggle: "Together We'll Win." It's a big shirt, but not big enough for his tummy. Look at it pop out there, all hairless and gleaming in the bright lights of the gym. Who knew the old boy could run so fast. We're gonna win this game of indoor flag football because Harry is a lot quicker than he looks and he just won't hear of losing. It was the same at the sand castle competition yesterday. That was fun too. Man, did we all get hammered. It's a little early in the day for that right now, though. We'll probably start a little before five this afternoon, it being raining and all. I'm glad it rained. I didn't want to go on the stupid paintball thing. Not with guys like Gefner, McDougal, and Spitz. I could see one of them sneaking up on a person and launching a paintball into their face. Whoops, sorry you're blind, man. I'm sure you'll get over it in a couple of weeks. Wait. Here comes Harry and he's got the flag. His face is the color of ripe cherries. Nobody better get in his way. A big kid, determined to win, victory in sight. Everybody is screaming. A big hot room full of people who are all part of one big thing. God, I love these guys. I wonder if I can see Jane Hartnett in her bikini later at the water polo match. . . .*

Even retired people need friends. In fact, one of the great detriments of a real postcareer existence is how lonely it can be. I have a theory that people die right after they quit working because some part of them quickly becomes too lonely to live. How many stories have you heard that end, "What a shame. He worked for forty years to make his nut and then keeled over on the fourteenth green six weeks after he called it quits." It's probably why your garden-variety mogul works until he's 90, or 190 if he can arrange the cybernetic implants. The idea of doing nothing isn't so bad. It's doing it without a social context that kills something in the spirit, particularly in the soul of someone who has been part of an organization for any period of time.

That is why the company retreat—also known as the boondoggle by those who diminish its importance—is so crucial to our overall effort. It is the employed person's way of enjoying all the perks of a first-class vacation club just like the ones that reside around the world for the terminally retired—but without the attendant shiftless anomie that surrounds the actual places themselves. It is one of the great joys of company life, if you minimize the risks and maximize the gains.

This last consideration is key. Handled in the wrong way, the boondoggle can be a career-destroying event, or at least highly unpleasant. Serious dangers lie in its unstructured nature, for in social groups, structure provides self-definition, understanding of individual roles and codes of dress and conduct, and

## Getting Invited to the Boondoggle: Tips for Borderline Players

1. Stay in touch with the team that puts together the production end of the retreat; they will hear about it first;

2. If there's any question about your attendance, start snuffling around work-related aspects. These include speeches, slide shows, notes for executives, booking of entertainment, and planning of team-building games, etc.;

3. You may have to work such an event for several years before you make it into the inner circle; be happy you're near the action;

4. If nobody on your level is at the event, you DON'T want to be there; being the odd man out is worse than being home with the rest of the plebes.

safety within the confines of mutually agreed-upon norms. Without those in place, anything can happen and often does. So while there is fun and freedom in that dissolution of formal interpersonal construct, the illusion that what happens at the boondoggle, as in Vegas, stays there, can be absolutely cataclysmic long-term.

There are so many bad things that can happen to you on an offsite, which is the polite term for the event. Let's think of as many as we can. I believe you will notice a theme here, by the way. When people get together far away from home, one of the ways they modulate their sense of dislocation and insecurity is with booze, in quantities that subsume the normal personality and free the inner stupid person.

You could disgrace yourself either in front of the people you work for or the people who work for you. I had a great old boss once who couldn't hold his liquor. Every time we'd get out of town he'd have exactly one scotch and then morph into a sleazy, drooling sex maniac. Not that he'd do anything about it. Walter was too good a guy, really. It was more like being with a thirteen-year-old boy who just discovered that girls had breasts. We'd sit in the hotel bar at a comfortable table and he'd have his drink and Mr. Hyde would appear, with disordered hair and tiny, red eyes and drool on his chin. "Lookit that one," he'd say, leering at a perfectly ordinary woman who looked like she just got off work at a local accounting office. "Yum-yum," he would conclude, moving on to his next fantasy date. I just let him devolve. There was no way I could slap him upside his head and say, "Walt, cut it out." But it made me see him in a different light not completely consonant with the goals of the offsite.

You could do what I did one time in Houston. It was with my friend Jack. Jack is six and a half feet tall and weighs about 220. He can drink an ocean of poison and all that happens to him is that his eyes get very small and his face turns the color of a ripe tomato. Beyond that, he looks quite dignified. He also gets rather truculent. Anyway, we got through our afternoon meetings, and Jack sidled up to me and said, "Come on. Let's turn this town into a parking lot," one of his favorite exhortations. We went out to a variety of drinking establishments and nothing much happened, except that we drank a lot. I matched him, martini for martini, and I am not of German/Irish descent, nor of his size. At one place, we nearly got into some trouble when Jack discovered a large group of college football players drinking beer and hooting like gibbons. He decided they were "assholes" and proceeded to walk slowly around the bar bumping into them, one by one, on purpose. At that time, he had graduated to his next favorite trope, which is, "We're gonna wreck this joint." I want you to keep in mind that Jack was a big vice president in one of the largest multinational corporations in the world, the head of the Human Resources function, in fact, and, when at home and in the pocket, one of the very best guys you could ever hope to meet.

Anyhow, I got us out of there without a fight and we went to our next place, which was not quite a strip joint but happened to have a large number of girls on hand. People were dancing. In retrospect, I think people were dancing with other people they actually knew, but that didn't occur to me at the time. I selected an attractive young woman and asked her to dance. I can't remember if she said yes or not but we did dance, sort of, for a little while . . . until a couple of guys who knew her returned from the men's room. Either that, or they were bouncers, I can't really remember. All I know is that suddenly there were a lot of very tall, very wide fellows around me, and there was some yelling, and then my pal picked me up and carried me out of the club and threw me into a cab that was providentially waiting outside.

"Well," he said, looking at me with a level of sobriety that frightens me to this day. "That was close."

That very night, in fact, a group of guys from Lorimar ended their careers. They went to a club, got hammered, and began touching the girls. Strip clubs are places of dubious propriety, of course, but they have very, very strict rules of their own that protect the workers and visitors alike, and chief among those is that no one, for any reason, is allowed to handle the talent. They were arrested, taken to jail, and that was that for them. It was the talk of the town. See how I still remember the name of the company they worked for?

Sometimes I get a little shiver when I think how close I came that very night. There but for the grace of a really unreliable and toasted friend go I, huh? And you, too, if you don't watch out.

One of my favorite tales, quite legendary in a long-dead incarnation of my company, is about the time when Norbert Lacy, who was our executive VP of investor relations, decided that he didn't want to go to bed, in spite of the long day of boondoggling behind him. It was about 2 AM, and down the hall from him at the offsite resort was the room of Joan Harbison, the vice president of marketing and every pin-striped porker's corporate wet dream. Joan was really pretty, very smart, didn't mind a short skirt now and then, and smelled a whole lot better than any other senior officer.

So Norbert got a nice, big bottle of cold champagne from his honor bar and took a shower, donned one of those big, plushy bathrobes that they give you at such places, and headed down the hall in his bare feet. Ding dong. Rang Joan's bell. She came to the door. "What is it, Norbert?" she said, quite patient, for indeed Joan knew precisely what "it" was. "I thought maybe you'd like a little nightcap," says Norbert, with a friendly smile. Joan laughed in his face and then sent him back to his room. I'm afraid she couldn't help but tell a couple of trusted friends afterward. And of course each of us promised not to tell anybody about it. I hope you'll show the same restraint, too.

People feel guilty in the morning after they do these kinds of things. And eventually, most of us get to a certain age when we don't do them anymore. Few actually commit atrocities they need to genuinely feel ashamed of forever. Most of us just act like schmucks. Do that kind of stuff often enough, however, and you lose your right to continue your bogus retirement.

None of these tales even takes in the perils of the number one boondoggle location in the world—Las Vegas. There are so many ways to hurt yourself in Vegas! I personally hate the place, possibly because as I rounded the turn at forty I lost the ability to lose money and have fun at the same time. I once saw an industry nabob of some sort lose $400,000 on one hand of faro. I thought I would barf, and it wasn't even my money. The waste! Think of what humanity could have done with that money! Or, if humanity couldn't get its hands on it, how about what I could have done with it? For his part, Ralph smiled, stood up, tossed a few $1,000 chips at the lowly, and cruised out of there to have another couple of drinks. I saw him again later in the evening, playing roulette. I heard from people that by the end of the year this mogul had lost more than $5 million while gambling. I guess that's chump change to some people. But it's not what you'd call wealth creation.

Me, I feel like hanging myself if I lose $200. So I don't gamble anymore. If you don't gamble in Vegas, there are really only two things you can do. One involves going to the convention floor. The other doesn't. Neither one is my idea of retirement. If it's not yours, either, you might want to wait for the occasions in Palm Springs, Sanibel Island, or Hilton Head. People still get into trouble there. But they tend to get home in one piece.

There are other challenges to face in these more sedate locations, of course. In place of gambling, boozing and other fun

EXECUTRICK:

## Not Hurting Yourself in Vegas

*1.* Eat an apple every day;

*2.* Get to bed by 3:00;

*3.* Take good care of yourself, you belong to me;

*4.* But seriously, eat food. Drink water. Go to some meetings. Establish a bedtime. Remember yourself!

*5.* Don't do things you don't want to do;

*6.* Call home regularly;

*7.* No more than 12 drinks in any 24-hour period.

stuff you don't want to tell your pastor about, there is the monolithic organizational activity that must be understood and conquered in one way or another if your boondoggle is to be a success. It's the ultimate game for the retired person, real or otherwise, one that takes hours of preparation, eats up a huge part of the day, and generally ends with eating and drinking.

It's called golf.

I'd like to try an experiment. Tell me if you find this funny.

*This man goes to confession and says, "Forgive me, Father, for I have sinned." The priest asks if he would like to confess his sins and the man replies that he used the "F-word" over the weekend.*

*The priest says, "Just say three Hail Marys and watch your language in the future, my son."*

*The man replies that he would like to confess as to why he said the "F-word." The priest sighs. "Please continue, my son," he says.*

*"Well, Father, I played golf on Sunday with my buddies instead of going to church."*

*The priest says, "And you got upset over that and swore?"*

*The man replied, "No, that wasn't why. On the first tee I duck-hooked my drive into the trees."*

*The priest said, "And that's when you swore?"*

*"No, Father, it wasn't. When I walked up the fairway, I noticed my ball got a lucky bounce and I had a clear shot to the green. However, before I could hit the ball, a squirrel ran by and grabbed my ball and scurried up a tree."*

"And that is most certainly when you swore," the priest interjected.

The man replied, "No, Father! Because right then an eagle flew by and caught the squirrel in its sharp talons and flew away."

The priest gasped. "And that must be when you swore!"

"No, because the eagle flew over the green and the dying squirrel let go of my golf ball and it landed within five inches of the hole."

"Christ," said the priest. "Please don't tell me you missed the fucking putt."

The thing is? I do. What that means to me is that golf has crept into my spirit, even though I do not play it, even though I have been on a course no more than a dozen times, during which I swung a club only, say, 1,500 times and lost several hundred golf balls in the process. And yet, I recognize the importance of golf, or golflike activities, in the working retirement we are constructing for ourselves. What we are contemplating can't be done without it, or something like it. No golf, no glory.

A word of reassurance for those about to skip to the next chapter: This will not be a discussion about golf, or at least wholly so. Unless you read golf magazines that discuss the position of your wrist during a backswing on uneven terrain, I don't expect you to stay with me just by talking about golf itself. No, I will be using golf as a metaphor, which is pretty much what most writers do with it anyhow if they expect to retain the attention of any normal person, even one in business.

In fact, the game instantly makes people who talk about it, let alone play it, boring. Even Alice Cooper is dull when he shows up in jodhpurs or sarongs, or whatever silly thing people wear on the golf course. I personally find it very depressing to be forced to consider the similarities between tattooed hipsters in stingy-brim hats and guys like Bob Hope and my dentist.

Unfortunately, it's hard to ignore golf altogether, and if you intend to, you'd better find yourself another game that confers some social benefit that builds your retirement effort. Try to find one that, like golf, can be played while drinking.

## EXECUTRICKS:
### Things You Can Do if You Don't Play Golf

1. Set up your own foursome that can't play and enjoy driving the cart around in the fresh air; make sure to FOLLOW the last serious foursome!

2. Hang around the nineteenth green wearing golf clothes and act like you played;

3. Establish a poker game for guys who don't play;

4. Take a lesson. When people ask you if you played, you say, "Nah. Rotator cuff. But I took a lesson." That's a respectable position.

There are, of course, many wonderful things that go on at boondoggles. I don't want you to think that they are all fraught with moral and physical dangers.

There are the meetings and presentations where people get to show their best stuff, and the award presentations, where those who have achieved excellence get tiny plaques or statuettes attesting to their achievements. These mean a lot, although not as much as some might think. I remember calling a guy after one of our most emotional management meetings, and asking how it felt to be the top Sales guy in the Great Northwest. "You

---

## EXECUTRICKS:
### *"Working" Your Boondoggle*

*1.* Remember this is part of your retirement package; don't work it too hard;

*2.* Mingle with everybody: part of the bosses' job at a retreat is to mix with people like you;

*3.* Don't overwork your chances to talk with the big dogs, but being in the vicinity is often enough;

*4.* No team-building event is too stupid to be taken seriously, but don't be a nerd;

*5.* Never lose a game on purpose, even to a boss, but no sack dances;

*6.* This is all about fun, believe it or not. So, you know, have some. Funsters at one boondoggle are invited to the next.

---

called me at a good time, Bing," he said to me. "I was just packing up my office. They fired me yesterday." I was speechless. How could a guy win a gold star one week and be toast the next? "Reorg of the department," he said. So much for the long-term value of awards.

There are the speakers they hire to amuse, entertain, and enlighten us. I recall one year when we brought James Carville in to speak to the top twenty people in our corporation. He arrived kind of late and joined us after dinner, looking kind of whipped. We all sat around the fire and he listened to us spin some stories and chatted about politics a little bit. Then he went home. I've wanted a job like that ever since. Let me know if you hear of one.

There is also ample opportunity to use the splendid facilities that exist in abundance at all the places to which companies retreat . . . the terrific food, twenty-four/seven . . . the gyms and running paths . . . the tennis courts and bride trails . . . the hikes in the desert . . . the off-road ATV excursions and trips where you get to fire guns and shoot skeet . . . and of course the spas.

A word about these emporia of bodily wellness. They include swimming pools, saunas, steam baths, weight rooms, massage tables staffed by sensuous, oil-bearing therapists, soft music, and lights. They are wonderful respites from the hubbub and hurly-burly of the game we all play. But they contain a serious threat to the mental health of any individual who frequents them. There is the possibility—remote if you deal with it

appropriately—of seeing one of your colleagues or senior officers naked.

Recent research into this area shows that the worst crises of
the human spirit attend the following events:

- ▶ Death of a loved one/pet;

- ▶ Moving residences;

- ▶ Divorce;

- ▶ Loss of job;

- ▶ Seeing your boss naked.

This is most true if your boss is male and over fifty-eight
years of age. Equally unsettling is the fact that while you are seeing more of this individual than you ever cared to, he is seeing
you as well.

I know a woman who is the head of communications for a
large manufacturing company headquartered in the Midwest.
Let's call her Louise. She was at a boondoggle with her ultra–
senior management not long ago, and had just had a swim,
sauna, and massage. Emerging from the shower into the locker
room wrapped demurely in a towel, she ran into a board member who had been invited to attend the event. "She was stark
naked," Louise told me over drinks one evening. She took a
long pull on her vodka. "I'll never forget it. She just stood there
talking about corporate issues and the company's prospects in

the new year and she was just . . . hanging out all over the place. She's not an attractive woman. And she's not in shape, either. It was pretty horrible."

I knew exactly what she meant. At the beginning of my career, I worked for a guy I'll call Jason. He liked to put people through the wringer. One day he scheduled a "group workout" at the gym of the resort to which we had retreated for our boondoggle. We sweated and threw medicine balls around and ran a little, all in the name of building that team. And after, as we were all getting ready to go out and hurl or collapse, Jason said, "Come on, you guys! Let's take a steam!" and he dropped his shorts and went into the steam room completely naked. So we all went in there, clutching our little wraps as best we could, and sat down on the wooden benches. It was very hot. Jason was very naked. And then he said, "What are you guys, sissies? Get rid of those towels!" so we all had to drop our coverings and just sit there, starkers. The benches grew even hotter. We sweated. It was very silent. Every now and then, we tried to talk a little business, but it was too, too weird. I tried not to look at the other guys. I knew they were trying not to look at anybody else. We were used to seeing each other in business garb, defined by the quality and style of our costume. Now . . . who were we? A bunch of naked men who didn't know each other. That's what I call team building. Not.

Come to think of it, this same president, for that was his title, also introduced into our boondoggle a not-uncommon dimension for which you must remain alert. Jason liked to set up life-threatening events to test the mettle of the people who worked for him. One year he nearly got somebody killed on a white-water rafting trip. The following summer he forced a bunch of executives on a boondoggle of his making to form teams, then dropped each grouping into the middle of the desert near Palm Springs, but I mean *way* out. Their job was to get back to the resort hotel with no water and no compass. The first team back would be declared the winner, presumably garnering a trophy, bragging rights, and potential career advancement.

Several hours went by. The sun beat down. The vice president in charge of the West Coast region began to feel kind of sick, and pretty soon it was clear that she was well on her way to a potentially lethal case of sunstroke. Her team noted her condition, had a discussion, then took a vote. It was decided, with some regret, that Carolyn was slowing them down too much and that, if they ministered to her or waited around for help to come, they would most certainly lose the contest, with unknown results, given Jason's nature. So they found a rock near the side of the road in whose shade Carolyn could lie down, put up some kind of a flag, and took off. I believe they came in second. Carolyn was eventually found, brought to the hospital, hydrated, and returned to the resort to the cheers of the multitude. She left the company about four months later. Sometimes it takes that long, you know, to find another job when you've decided you can no longer work somewhere.

Offsites often take place near some form of nature. Nature is not inherently hospitable to people like you and me. So if you have any doubts about whether you'd like to hang glide, or go into a 135-degree sweat lodge, or be dropped onto the top of a mountain to ski down its double black diamond slopes, bag the character test and head for your room. "I was e-mailing" is a perfectly good response to "where were you on the white-water rafting trip?"

Death follows any worthwhile retirement at a respectful distance. It's not part of the basic package.

# 8

# The Working Trick

*Never do things others can do and will do if there are
things others cannot do or will not do.*
AMELIA EARHART

*A perpetual holiday is a good working definition of hell.*
GEORGE BERNARD SHAW

*Some things can't be planned for. At ten this morning, the phone rings. It's Bob. "Come up," he says. I have always dreaded those words. Not, "Hi, listen, there are a couple of things we need to go over," or "When you have a minute, I'd like to get together." No, just "Come up." It always means work. Not the kind of work you can think about, parse out in your mind, and then delegate to maintain your ongoing retirement; no, the kind of work that you have to roll up your mental and physical sleeves for and push up the hill until it's well and truly in position. I go up. "We are merging with Thanatos," says Bob. He looks tired. "Merging," I reply. I have always hated that word. There is no such thing as a merger. A merger is a polite word for something far more frightening. A sale. The ingestion of one company by another. One fish swallowing the other. "Who is merging who," I ask Bob. "I'll be the COO of the new operation," he says. "Lester Crepescule will be the chief executive. I want you to work with those guys to make sure the whole transition comes out right as far as we're concerned, and by 'we' I of course mean me." "When?" I ask. My stomach has taken a sharp left and headed for Tucson. "When?" says Bob. He looks annoyed. "Now, man. Right now."*

---

I wish I could say the story above was a once-in-a-lifetime event, but it isn't. I mean, it hasn't been. The circumstances may change. To a certain extent, it depends on the rhythm of the investment banks. Sometimes they want to sell you. Other times, they want you to buy somebody. Eventually, the CFO advises everybody to suck it up and do what the banks want. Chaos follows. Chaos is the opposite of retirement.

Likewise, as solid and immutable as one's management structure might appear, people die, or fall from favor, or move along to their next iteration. This inevitably precipitates the requirement for short-term labor to reestablish equilibrium. Equilibrium is what it's all about.

Whatever the precise situation, those in the midst of a happy and fulfilled mid-career retirement will need to negotiate the requirement for forceful, sustained effort now and then if their bucolic status is not to be doomed by constant inundations of flotsam, followed almost inevitably by jetsam.

I don't mean to be flippant. The truth is, I find this chapter as odious to write as you will probably find it to read. But it's necessary. Let us therefore dispatch it in the same spirit with which you will be forced to face this challenge to your executive status—quickly, decisively, with the smallest amount of stomach lining lost as possible. Then we can get back to our dilatory routine.

Our goal at this juncture is clear: to work with maximum power for the shortest amount of time possible. This kind of labor is quite different from the grinding, tedious type we have dedicated ourselves to avoiding. Instead, it is short, intense, and concentrated, with a tremendous, satisfying release at its climax.

It's no wonder that certain people who can't get much sex become addicted to this kind of work instead.

But what do we mean by the phrase "this kind of work"? So far we've been vaguely disrespectful toward the entire idea of work, identifying it as anything that interrupts our lunch. This thinking is only correct up to a certain point, and we have now reached that point . . . the moment when we must drop "work" and actually work.

It is not out of place, however, to ask a pertinent question: what is work? Isn't learning to ski work? It's hard. You could

## Things That Are Not Work and Why

| NOT WORK | WHY |
|---|---|
| Procedural meeting | Vague requirement for deliverables; tool for indolence and procrastination |
| Dining | Too sensory; work could be done elsewhere |
| Honking on phone | High BS quotient |
| PowerPoint | Puts off actual thinking |
| Playing golf | Come on. Seriously. |
| Sniffing cheese/wine | Not unless you are paid for cheese sniffing or wine snorkling |
| Painting landscapes | Not unless you are Van Gogh |

get injured. But no, it isn't. Certainly there are certain aspects of learning to ski that are worklike. But it is not work, or at least the kind of work we're talking about. Nor, by the way, is attending six months of committee meetings to agree on the content of the chairman's presentation at the annual gathering of dowagers and skanky retirees that make up the vast majority of attendees at the company's annual meeting. What goes down the night before that event, however, may be real work indeed. It depends on just how crazy your chairman can get.

It is therefore important for us to correctly ascertain when the moment has arrived that we must pull the consummate trick out of our bag of executricks, and actually work for a living, producing something that has meaning to the organization, so that afterward we can go hang upside down on our favorite tree without shame, guilt, or timetable.

I would like to suggest that the word "work"—the kind that kicks us into genuine action—may be defined as follows:

1. You get paid for it and if you don't do it you don't get paid at all.*

---

*You will note that artists, musicians, novelists, inventors, philosophers, and others who labor in obscurity would not be included in this category. I am not suggesting that what these people do is not work, but rather that they are entrepreneurs investing effort for a future payout of some kind—money, fame, or, in the case of someone like Nietzsche or Van Gogh—the momentary peace of mind that comes with the immersion in the work itself. Beethoven was never confused on this issue. His head was filled with music even after he went deaf, and he never failed to dun his clients for payment.

**2.** Sustained physical and mental effort is required, along with certain professional expertise accumulated over a period of time.

**3.** Somebody told you to do it.

**4.** The need for excellence, accuracy, timeliness—for "getting it right the first time"—is extreme and not imaginary.

**5.** You have to keep doing it until it's done; if you quit before it is defined as finished and acceptable by others (not simply by yourself), you lose power, status, and possibly your bonus.

**6.** Completion may be attended by a certain feeling of personal fulfillment not solely obtained through the experience of room service, no matter how fine that might be.

This last point is key. After all we've been through, we should really admit the truth. The brandishing of our skills, the accomplishment of miracles, the execution of impossible strategies, the feel of the sweat on our brow, knowing that it will soon be wiped away by our talent, verve, and drive—there is truly nothing like it. It's all the more wonderful because, if we have done everything else correctly, it occurs so rarely and lasts for so short a sweet time.

Right, then. We have our work. It has arrived. And now we're going to kick its ass. I like to view this as a twelve-step process, since that method has been notably successful in helping people exorcise other demons and move on with their lives.

These twelve steps are far less emotional and do not require appeals to a Higher Power. You are the one in control.

**Step One: Receive orders.** The alarm may be sounded in a variety of ways, and you must attune yourself to hear it. We receive so many instructions, requests, and demands in any given workweek. The majority, as we have demonstrated, may be turned easily from Work into "work," either through delegation, bureaucratization, shirking, procrastination, or a variety of other means that you should be well versed in by now. But the actual moment in which the general miasma begins to form in the shape of a mushroom must not be missed.

The tool best suited to inform you that that moment has in fact arrived is right beneath your belt. It's called your gut.

Here's how it works: A piece of labor appears. The natural reaction on the part of any executive is to cringe. This could be the big one, the event that screws you up, twists you around, makes everybody suddenly become aware of what a bimbo you are. Then, for most of us on this particular hajj, reality kicks in. Our talent for making others do our bidding rises like cream to the top of the issue. We revert to business as usual and reassert our basic status of stasis and sangfroid.

For those in touch with the little man or woman who resides inside their gut, that paradigm is toast. The tiny, self-preserving entity inside you should be screaming. Every attempt to tell it to shut up and defer to the usual deadheads and slackers who are hanging around in there will be to no avail. No, the seasoned warrior will immediately have a different reaction than the droid who is chugging along doing what comes naturally.

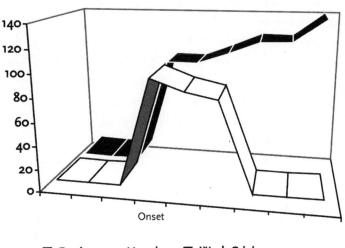

## Gut Reaction to Onset of Actual Work

□ **Business as Usual**   ■ **Work Crisis**

If you don't know enough to follow the thick black line upward and heed that small and not-very-silent voice . . . well, there's nothing I can do to help you, Spud. The back tables at industry rubber chicken dinners are full of you guys.

**Step Two: Ascertainment.** The horn has sounded. We are no longer dealing with a political or bureaucratic matter, amenable to procedure, discussion, and other quasi-solutions offered by organizational wheezing. No, this is in fact a military exercise, one that must be executed with speed and distinction. There's a reason why business types like to read biography and history. Sure, it aggrandizes our generally fatuous vocation. But it also gives us a useful metaphor to guide us.

So . . . What kind of battle are we talking about? We certainly have a variety to choose from. There are long-term campaigns like the Battle of Britain, which was won by the civilian population of London by just hanging in there and refusing to be conquered. There's a lot of time for bangers and mash during that kind of thing, but retirement it's not.

Such exchanges should be transformed into short, hard-pitched battles whenever possible so you can get back to "work." The revolutionary bourgeoisie who founded the United States of America had that kind of thing down cold, making themselves a total pain to the Redcoats from the moment they threw that first box of tea into Boston Harbor. Eventually they won because they didn't play by the rules of good sportsmanship as defined by the dominant power.

Not every war is conducted as a series of intense skirmishes, of course. The good news about more sustained conflagrations is that they almost immediately morph into a weird, scary form of everyday life. The doomed Israelites who were trapped by the Roman army on top of a mountain called

## What Kind of Conflict?

**1.** The Battle of Bunker Hill, in which a bunch of feisty patriots challenge the power of the greatest empire in the world? Reverse takeovers are like that.

**2.** The Battle of Actium: Octavian versus Antony, two great powers fight it out at sea, and only one of them has appropriate equipment and management, two corporations coming to blows for the same piece of business. Hopefully, you're not the ones being led by a mad Egyptian sexpot leading your CEO around by his Johnson.

**3.** D-Day, a massive, secret exercise where thousands are deployed merely to gain a foothold on enemy soil. Sneaking up on a big deal, you might have to plan an entire explosive effort in the dark, springing the trap shut at a moment's notice.

**4.** The 100 Years' War: Medieval horror. Lots die. Nothing is resolved. You are being invaded by McKinsey. Ultimately, they will leave. But the ground will be scorched for generations.

**5.** Thermopolae: Try to be the Persians.

Masada in suburban Jerusalem had plenty of time to hang around, raise families, and make believe everything was normal while the Romans down below sweated in the heat and waited them out. Sure, eventually they died. But doesn't everybody?

Most of the time, thank goodness, we'll be dealing with

brief, brutal engagements that confirm clear winners and los-ers. That's the game we're best at anyhow.

**Step Three: Evaluate terrain and timeline.** Let's say, just for argument's sake, the deal is that your boss is leaving and you're getting a new one. Thinking clearly, you immediately ascertain the following:

▶ The old boss's agenda has suddenly shrunk in impor-tance and should be dealt with immediately so that it will not stand in the way of the actual business at hand, i.e., transitioning;

▶ The new boss will need a clear, unbiased point of view about operations that is consonant with your own best interests;

▶ You are the one best suited to provide that service;

▶ Any person or thing that stands in your way in this regard must be (1) distracted, (2) removed from the prem-ises, or (3) killed;

▶ You will need support to provide documents, briefing papers, situation analyses, and other bushwah that will impress the new chief; for this some internal resources must be mustered;

▶ Speed is of the essence.

There are other considerations. Only you, after all, know the exact circumstances of your employment and the particular situation that presents the challenge. The need to comprehend and assess, however, is universal.

**Step Four: Appoint appropriate point personnel and deploy existing forces.** You can't do everything yourself—in comparison with your normal routine, where you basically can't do *anything* yourself.

If you've been following the program, however, you already have a cadre of dedicated, hardworking people who are used to doing your bidding and then some. The difference here is that you're the one on point. You're not simply there to issue direc-

---

### EXECUTRICK:
#### Reeling in Your People

1. Call them in;

2. Inform them of the State of War;

3. Raise level of gravity;

4. Establish change of tone;

5. Distribute focused assignments;

6. Set up demand for heightened communications;

7. Execute traitors, spies, and screwups immediately.

---

tions and receive data between facials. You are up front, guiding, sending others to their doom, positioning troops to the right and left flanks, if you have flanks. Make sure that every person you can muster is cutting the mustard. While you may have grown used to allowing other people to attend the planning sessions and interface with senior management, this is not the time for that. This is war. Things could go south while you're up north. Control, baby. You have relinquished most of it as you ventured up the lazy river. Reel it in. Take it back. You need it now.

It is equally important, by the way, that any person to whom you report also has firm control over *you* for a change, as in:

▶ Knowing where you are;

▶ Holding you accountable for clear deliverables;

▶ Able to reach out and touch you on demand in all appropriate places;

▶ Aware of your availability for emotional and spiritual support. In a time of crisis, there's a lot of being there and listening.

This last is quite important. During wartime, people need to feel the warm and comforting sensation that they are not alone, that they are surrounded by people they can trust. So be trustworthy for a change. We're playing with live ammo. You may even be asked to take a bullet for your captain, and you are not permitted to resort to your usual tactic of throwing somebody else in its path this time.

**Step Five: Hire mercenaries.** Think of a chain, strong only as its weakest link. There are people who can fortify that potential gap fast and well, and then fade back into the underbrush from whence they came. They're called consultants. Major acquisitions, mergers, and other natural disasters often require Hessians to provide logistical support, event management, media relations, even financial analysis. Investment banks, for instance, would be nowhere if CFOs didn't immediately give the outside A-team a call when something real was coming down. The same is true for out-of-house counsel, expenses for which often far outstrip internal costs of actual Law departments in active corporations.

A keen eye must be fixed, however, on the issue of whether the costs of hired guns continue to match the benefits, the value of which tend to decline over time.

You will note here that while consultant costs remain relatively fixed, the value they provide after the initial blitz decreases dramatically, declining, in fact, into negative territory as they gum up the works and block organizational solutions to problems. This all drains resources that could once again be allotted to lunch.

In this phase, outside counselors, assassins, spies, and toadies stick around mostly as security blankets for bad managers

## A Cost Consultant's Benefit Analysis

who have lost the ability to hire and cultivate decent staff, or who want the deniability provided by such people. "We've got Brewster & Snodgrass working on this!" has extended the life span of more than one mid-level officer whose bosses have lost faith in his perspicacity. That's not you. Use them then lose them.

**Step Six: Secure the King.** Many a war has been lost when, in the midst of an otherwise successful campaign, the executive officer gets cut down. There are a host of bad things that can happen to his retainers after the death of a monarch, up to and including enslavement in a hostile corporate culture and even, in extreme cases, career death.

I once engaged in a protracted crusade for the acquisition of an entirely new territory that was coveted by my well-loved senior officer. For several years, he had in his mind a grand vision of a virgin land occupied by our troops and colonized by our citizens. And so, after a time, it did come to pass. During the ensuing reorganization that always follows such conflicts, my Duke's boss, who was an actual Prince imported from a large consulting organization, decided that existing nobility from the acquired corporation was better suited to serve his interests. My Lord was assigned duties in a small castle just inside the border of Siberia, upon which all those who owed him fealty were cast to the winds. The fact that I told him this would happen was little comfort to me, and the ride I was forced to make over the frozen terrain back to the Kremlin in Moscow was one of the most harrowing of my life. It's nice here now, I'm pleased to say. Still miss Bill, though, now and then.

If an important piece of work could potentially destabilize your boss, take any steps you can to safeguard the font from which all good things flow to you. Keep him informed of the dangers to his crown. Kill his adversaries, if you can. Try to stand in the way of his own self-destructive impulses.

**Step Seven: Keep the information flowing.** Great data flow is essential for success. Most believe they have dispatched their responsibility in that area if they keep their boss informed with lame, tardy "heads-ups" that are simply warning alarms that let senior management know they're about to be flattened with a piano falling from a high window. Genuine communication is

## Constructing Good Communications

1. Demand it from below;

2. Provide it to those above;

3. Always accompany news of problems with potential solutions; they don't have to be good but a terrified, empty stare is not really appreciated by guys upstairs;

4. Keep expectations of victory low;

5. Do NOT convey horrible news, bad press clips, info about repulsive blogs, etc., to senior officers unless there is some utility; nobody needs to know what Gawker is saying about them;

6. Never allow bosses to shoot the messenger; do not shoot the messenger yourself;

7. Reward good communicators with excellent pay raises, bonuses.

constant, two-way, and assumes that all parties can only add value if they are informed of the real situation and all pertinent options pretty much moment to moment.

This does not mean abnegating responsibility for one's actions or simply passing the decision-making process up and down the reporting structure. It's making absolutely certain that if your CFO has been arrested for soliciting a circus clown, everybody knows about it before it hits the papers.

**Step Eight: Attack and win.** The moment inevitably comes when the report must be issued, the press conference held, the deal closed. At that juncture, all paper must be perfect, the right individuals must be properly positioned. Failure is not an option. It is amazing how much success at the critical moment is due to the sheer resolve to win. There are other factors that contribute to victory, but it's the sustained determination *not to lose* that has shaped world and business history.

The Carthaginians, for instance, beat the Romans over and over again in what came to be known as the Punic Wars. These contests went on for more than 100 years, which in those days equaled about five lifetimes for the citizen-soldiers of Rome, so many of whom died that they barely had time to marry and raise an offspring or two before getting hewn down by Hannibal or one of the other Barca family. And yet in the end Rome crushed its enemy and, in the first known use of a dirty bomb, salted its fields so that nothing could grow there for decades. Rome simply would not permit itself to be defeated.

Examples in the business universe are slightly less bloody but by no means less dramatic. One has only to look at some of the great deals of the last fifty years to see how often it is the most determined, demented, and hungry entity that ends up holding the bloody carcass of the beast it just *had* to consume.

Too many handbooks on corporate strategy forget this central fact: when it comes to work that matters, it is always the

**Components of Victory**

- Snacks, Booze
- Viciousness
- Supplies
- Planning
- Good Personnel
- Execution of Strategy
- Will to Win

inexorable, irrational, insatiable force that wins the day over the sentient, thoughtful, and reasonable.

**Step Nine: Make peace with opposing management.** If the war is ever to end, you have to convince your adversary that they came out a winner too. Then everybody can go back home feeling good about themselves and prepared to revert to everyday bureaucratic existence: that glow in the east that guides our glorious quest.

**Step Ten: Kill opposing management.** When Machiavelli wrote it long ago, everybody called him a bad guy. He didn't mean to be evil. In fact, he was by all reports a smart, funny, sexy fellow who loved life, liquor, and the company of intelligent and beautiful people. But he still advised killing those who opposed you after you've won the day. It's hard to see how he was wrong. They can't poke you in the eye if they're dead.

In nonmerger situations, this means ferreting out all those who did not perform as required during the recent fire drill and cutting them from the team. Players who can't play in the rain, can't play hurt, can't do their best work under pressure, just have to go. It's not personal. It's business. Send them to their great reward and start filling the gaps they leave with the kind of mofos you can count on when you're in the red zone.

**Step Eleven: Celebrate.** You've got the plastic. You're a winner. Live it up. Treat your friends and subordinates. Take your boss out for a couple of big, sweaty martinis. Go ahead. Make your day.

**Step Twelve: Return to normal.** Wow. Doesn't THAT feel nice? You've just earned the right to kick back in the corporate hammock until the next big wind blows. Enjoy that big tasty helping of impunity, too.

# The Ultimate Trick

*If you gaze for long into an abyss,*
*the abyss gazes also into you.*
FRIEDRICH NIETZSCHE

Who knows. Perhaps, when the last trumpet from Payroll blows, you'll feel content in the great green pasture that lies beyond work as we know it. I heard a story the other day about a guy who retired from the Army at fifty-two and is now in his eighties, traveling the world with his wife, reading, soaking it all in. People say that he was once a real hard-ass, but that now his attitude toward gay people, women, and all those with opinions other than his has softened. They say he's grown since the day he hung up his Glock. And he's happy.

Maybe so. It's a good story. I believe it, too. And yet . . .

I remember when my father-in-law had been retired for twenty years. He was seventy at the time. He mothballed his tie and jacket at fifty, having made just enough to live in a Florida golf community for the rest of his life.

Once a week, on Wednesday, he went to gas up his Buick. He

woke early, with the birds. The parking lot of the condo village was wet with dew. Salamanders scuttled back and forth on the golf paths. The sun was just peeping over the fairway, pale and mild.

After a light breakfast, he dressed in his best sweats, tied his running shoes tight, and hit the road. He was at the station by 7 AM. In his pocket was a small, dog-eared notebook, about half the size of a passport, maybe two inches wide and three inches tall. In it, Don had kept track of his weekly gas consumption for the last several decades. He would purchase gas, carefully noting the amount of gas the car consumed and the mileage at the time of the fueling operation. In the next column, he would calculate the mileage he had gotten during the interval since the last such operation. Then he would drive gingerly home and park the car in the slot he thought best, often quite far from the vestibule of the building, because it was less crowded and the chance that his pristine vehicle would get clipped by some other elderly driver was not quite so great.

One day, as he sat tying his Nikes for a trip into the 100-degree heat outdoors on some makeshift errand, he gazed up at me as I stood waiting to accompany him. "Stan," he said, pausing in his labors to fix me with the most serious expression with which he ever graced me. "I'm going to tell you something and I want you to remember it."

"Okay, Don," I said. I was unaccustomed to this degree of intensity from him. It sort of frightened me.

"Never retire," he said. He went back to tying his shoe for a moment, then looked at me again, and it was a different expression this time—softer, infinitely sad, filled with resignation and regret. "Never," he said again.

"Okay, Don," I said. He didn't have to tell me twice.

Working hard stinks sometimes. The stress engendered by our various inane occupations weighs us down, wrecks our peace of mind, makes us incapable of focusing on the big picture. Any tricks we can play, any clever stratagems we can execute to minimize the pain of a lifetime of strenuous effort should be hunted down like a prize stag and brought down for dinner.

But make no mistake. The alternative—perpetual idleness—is worse. Where there is work, there is hope. Where there is no work, there is nothing but meals at inappropriate hours, an obsessive need to talk about vegetables, and YouTube.

So study. Work hard to work less, and when you do have to work, keep the experience as brief as possible. But keep your deal together. Do not, in the end, get so tricky that you out-trick yourself. Dead careers produce dead people. How much better it is to squeeze the system until it coughs up all the good things to which we are almost entitled!

But it's not just about that. Or at least it doesn't have to be.

There is one aspect of your working retirement that we have yet to mention—and it happens to be a very real part of the post-employed lifestyle of off-the-grid geezers around the world.

Some call it philanthropy, in which those in need receive money, services, education, technology, or soup. One hears about the Art of Giving, in which those who have taken so much return something to society. Others indulge in the process of mentoring, in which people who presumably know something try to impart it to those who don't, creating a warm feeling in both parties. Whatever form of philanthropy it takes, the activity is a popular one for those in their declining years, and is one we may enjoy in the prime of our careers as well.

Incredibly, socially conscious, community-based activities are widely perceived not as departures from work, but as an integral part of it. That's why its pursuit is so rarely opposed by those who otherwise might keep an eye on your time clock. Right now in my corporation, which is as venal as most, people are tutoring inner-city children, volunteering for AIDS walks, organizing dinners for charity—and all on company time. Believe me, they're having more fun and feeling a lot better about themselves than they did when they were e-mailing their supply chain manager.

Even the most horrendous monsters we work for understand the philanthropic urge. In fact, the worse the mogul, the more sacred his heartfelt repentance phase. Henry Ford now serves humanity in the extended retirement attending his decease through the Ford Foundation, which he established to do good works after he was gone. Before he went to that great assembly line in the sky, however, he enjoyed a mutual-admiration relationship with Adolf Hitler, going so far as to receive the highest honor from the Reich in 1938. Most people don't know that, but they have heard of the Ford Foundation.

The robber barons who shot workers down on the picket lines of Pittsburgh, or squeezed their Chinese slave labor until they died building the railroads, now are memorialized in the names of the museums we visit, the universities and concert halls we attend, the hospitals in which we live or die.

Today, the people who control the vast majority of the globe's wealth may be seen in the Style sections of our newspapers funding this charity or another. A day does not pass when there isn't some tedious fund-raiser for a worthy cause. The fact that the ultrahumanitarians are sometimes rich, fatuous twits does not diminish the social value of their efforts.

The names of the giver-backers are a litany of the highest and mightiest of our culture. All of these collosi are distinguished not only by the size of their good works, but also by their status as exemplars of the life we seek. They are all retired while they are still working.

O brave new world, that has such people in it!

## FINAL EXECUTRICK:
### *Acknowledgments*

*1.* To all the guys at my corporation, who are constantly teaching me better ways to get the job done;

*2.* To my boss, possibly the only guy who tries as hard as I do to live the dream in spite of everything that's always going on;

*3.* To my longtime friend and eagle-eyed editor David Hirshey, who is clearly gleaning a few ideas from this book by delegating a nice amount of the associated work to . . .

*4.* . . . Kate Hamill, who, with class and distinction, made his semiretirement on this project possible;

*5.* To my publishers at Collins, Steve Ross and Margot Schupf, for making sure this book is in every airport, even those on the State Department's watch list;

*6.* And to my wife, Laura, for all the good ideas . . . and for making any kind of retirement, even a fake one, look appealing.

# ALSO BY STANLEY BING

**CRAZY BOSSES**
978-0-06-06073157-1 (hardcover)

**100 BULLSHIT JOBS . . .
AND HOW TO GET THEM**
978-0-06-073479-4 (hardcover)
978-0-06-073480-0 (paperback)

**SUN TZU WAS A SISSY**
Conquer Your Enemies, Promote Your
Friends, and Wage the *Real* Art of War
978-0-06-073477-0 (hardcover)
978-0-06-073478-7 (paperback)

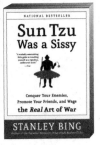

**WHAT WOULD MACHIAVELLI DO?**
The Ends Justify the Meanness
978-0-06-662010-7 (paperback)

**THE BIG BING**
Black Holes of Time Management,
Gaseous Executive Bodies, Exploding
Careers, and Other Theories on the
Origins of the Business Universe
978-0-06-052957-4 (paperback)

**THROWING THE ELEPHANT**
Zen and the Art of Managing Up
978-0-06-093422-4 (paperback)

Stanley Bing's books are also available in
HarperCollins e-book and downloadable audio formats.

 **Collins**    An Imprint of HarperCollins*Publishers*    www.harpercollins.com